THE ELEPHANT

Look for these and other books in the
Lucent Endangered Animals and Habitats series:

The Elephant
The Giant Panda
The Oceans
The Rhinoceros
The Shark
The Whale

Other related titles in the Lucent Overview series:

Acid Rain
Endangered Species
Energy Alternatives
Garbage
The Greenhouse Effect
Ocean Pollution
Oil Spills
Ozone
Pesticides
Population
Rainforests
Recycling
Vanishing Wetlands
Zoos

THE ELEPHANT

BY STUART P. LEVINE

Endangered
Animals &
Habitats

LUCENT BOOKS, INC.

SAN DIEGO, CALIFORNIA

Library of Congress Cataloging-in-Publication Data

Levine, Stuart P., 1968–
     The elephant / by Stuart P. Levine.
          p.   cm. — (Endangered animals & habitats)
     Includes bibliographical references (p.   ) and index.
     Summary: Presents an overview of elephants, how they have
become endangered, and what is being done to protect them from
extinction.
     ISBN 1-56006-522-2 (alk. paper)
     1. Elephants—Juvenile literature.   2. Endangered species—
Juvenile literature.   3. Wildlife conservation—Juvenile literature.
[1. Elephants. 2. Endangered species.]   I. Title.   II. Series.
QL737.P98L48   1998
599.67—dc21   97-28532
                                                                      CIP
                    ADULT ED   AC
                    QL 737
                    P98 L48
                    1998

Contents

Introduction

DURING THE LAST twenty years, world attention has been increasingly focused on the endangered status of animals and their habitats. Numerous conservation groups, nature magazines, and wildlife documentaries aim to increase awareness of the dangers facing the world's ecosystems. Much of this attention is focused on the largest of all land animals, the elephant. When humankind first evolved as a species, many different elephant-like creatures roamed all corners of the earth. Today, however, only two remain. The last living members of the Elephantidae family are the African elephant and the Asian elephant. According to scientists and conservationists, if current trends continue, these last two species may soon disappear as well.

The planet can support only a limited amount of life, sometimes called its "carrying capacity." It took approximately a million years for the human population to reach 1 billion. Just a few centuries later, that number had doubled. The most recent jump, from 4 to 5 billion, took only twelve years! Population trend researchers estimate that within the next fifty years, human numbers will have reached 10 to 12 billion. As these numbers rise, it is the animals and wild habitats of the world that must pay the price.

Elephants need an enormous amount of territory to flourish. Unlike most animals, which are adapted to relatively narrow environments, elephants are found in almost every type of terrain: grasslands, dense forests, coastal regions, and even the occasional desert. Even the adaptable elephant, though, is being squeezed into smaller and smaller patches of living space. The elephant cannot hope to compete with the technology and sheer numbers of the human species. As humans move into their territory, elephants following their natural migration routes trample homes and devour crops. Seen as a pest, elephants are often killed by local people to save their villages and their livelihoods.

In addition, elephants possess a unique anatomical feature that humans throughout history have found irresistible: ivory. The massive tusks of an elephant are used for foraging and protection, but, unfortunately, they have also been the cause of an unprecedented slaughter of the species during the last century. In just ten years, from 1979 to 1989, the African elephant population dropped from 1.3 million to 600,000, mostly from illegal ivory poaching. The Asian elephant typically has smaller tusks and has been less of a target for this trade. However, their native habitat has been destroyed on a much greater scale than that of their African cousins, and, as a result, their numbers stand at a mere 44,000.

As human populations increase, the habitat of the elephant has steadily decreased, leading to its endangerment.

Fortunately, in the last few years, efforts have begun to stabilize these populations and reduce the impact of humans. Both species are listed as "endangered" by the Endangered Species Act, passed by Congress in 1973, categorizing threatened species around the world, and the International Union for the Conservation of Nature's Red List, an internationally recognized list of threatened flora and fauna. A worldwide ban on ivory trade, initiated in 1989, has drastically reduced poaching. Establishment of national parks and wildlife reserves has also provided safe havens for elephants, where they can live unmolested by the pressures of human encroachment. Laws have been passed and money has been invested in the interests of preserving the species. However, these efforts may not be enough. The elephant's numbers have begun to stabilize, but the uphill battle for its preservation will have to be fought well into the next century.

Much of the protection recently afforded these animals exists on paper only. For example, in the late 1980s the U.S. Congress passed the African Elephant Conservation Act, which promises $5 million a year to elephant funds. However, actual contributions have fallen short of the designated total. In 1989 only $500,000 was actually allocated to the cause. In addition, many native preserves exist in name only. Without sufficient numbers of rangers to patrol these areas, poachers and farmers are still able to run unchecked through the territory.

The elephant populations of the world have suffered greatly for many years under the pressures of human expansion and human commerce. Will the situation improve quickly enough to reverse the damage that has been done? Though small numbers of people are attempting to counteract human injury to the environment, the future of the elephant will depend on the decisions of the rest of the human population. The elephant's chances at long-term survival currently hang in the balance, but scientists estimate its future will be irreversibly decided within the next fifty years.

1

About the Elephant

FROM THE TIME children start learning their first words in picture books, they can easily distinguish the elephant from all the other animals by its trunk, tusks, and massive gray body. Most people have grown up seeing elephants in the circus, in zoos, on TV, and in the movies. But until about thirty years ago, very little was known about the elephant beyond what it ate and where it lived. Since the 1960s, a continuous flood of elephant research has provided scientists with a huge amount of information on the animal's biology, social behavior, life span, evolution, breeding, and even the future of the species. In order to understand the complex issues surrounding the endangerment and conservation of elephants, it is important first to understand the nature of the animal itself.

The origin of the elephant

Scientists classify all living creatures in an internationally recognized scheme, or taxonomic structure. The elephant is a vertebrate, or backboned, mammal, the only nonextinct member of the order Proboscidea, in the family Elephantidae. Within the Elephantidae family there are two species: *Loxodonta africana* (African elephant), and *Elephas maximus* (Asian elephant). Researchers think that throughout history there have been more than six hundred separate species of proboscids (so named for its members' elongated, flexible snouts). The order is thought to have originated in Africa about 45 million years ago. The first member of this order was the *Moeritherium*, a small piglike creature that stood about two feet tall at the shoulder. This ancestor is thought to have lived in the lowlands of northern Egypt. Over the next 5 million years, the proboscideans migrated north across Europe, Asia, and even North America. Hundreds of elephant ancestors came and went. By the arrival of the Ice Age, about 1 million years ago, the only proboscids left were the mammoth, the mastodon, and our modern elephants.

Mastodons were found exclusively in North America. They were slightly smaller than elephants, standing almost ten feet at the shoulder. Cave drawings indicate that they lived alongside the Indians of North America for about one to two thousand years. While mastodons were in the same order as elephants, according to researcher Jeheskel Shoshani, they were in a different family and are not considered "true elephants."

Mammoths, on the other hand, are considered to have been "true elephants," as they were members of

A mastodon herd tramples through Manhattan Island during the Quaternary Age. Although the mastodon is similar to the elephant, they are in a different family.

the Elephantidae family. They were found throughout western Europe, Asia, and North America. The most well known of the mammoths was the woolly mammoth. This animal was actually shorter than a modern elephant, standing about nine feet at the shoulder, but its tusks were up to 50 percent longer, some reaching nearly sixteen feet. Because conditions in the frozen tundra of Siberia were ideal for preservation, more than forty partial or complete woolly mammoth carcasses have been unearthed and studied. During the eighteenth and nineteenth centuries alone, between forty thousand and sixty thousand mammoth tusks were collected in Siberia. Unfortunately, few of these still exist intact. Even this extinct species has been exploited by humans. Most of the tusks were made into billiard balls, piano keys, chess pieces, and assorted jewelry.

For at least the last ten thousand years, the world has only known two separate species of elephant: the African and the Asian. While similar in many ways, these two species have some very distinct differences.

The African elephant

Loxodonta africana, or the African elephant, is found in several regions throughout the continent after which it is named. In recent years, *Loxodonta* has received the attention of the world because of its dwindling numbers. Today there are approximately 600,000 African elephants in the world. Some believe this represents a stable population and that measures to protect them are unnecessary. Others argue that while elephants are locally overabundant in certain areas, it is impossible to ignore the fact that the overall population has dropped by a staggering amount. As recently as 1979 there were an estimated 1.3 million African elephants. This unprecedented decline is attributed primarily to poaching, or illegal hunting, and habitat loss.

African elephants are distinguished from Asians in several ways. The most noticeable difference is the ears. Africans' ears are much larger and are conveniently shaped like the continent of their origin. The African elephant is typically larger than the Asian and has a concave (or

The African Elephant

- Average length: 20–24.5 feet
- Average weight: More than 6 tons
- Potential life span: 60 years
- Amount of food consumed each day: Up to 300 lbs.
- Amount of water consumed each day: 19–24 gallons
- Gestation period: 22 months
- Average weight of an elephant calf: 265 lbs.

Source: World Wildlife Fund.

dipped) back. Both males and females have external tusks and are usually less hairy than their Asian cousins.

Within the *Loxodonta* species, most scientists recognize two distinct subspecies, or races. The first is the bush African elephant (*Loxodonta africana africana*), the largest of all the elephants. In fact, it is the largest land animal in the world, standing on average thirteen feet at the shoulder and weighing approximately 15,400 pounds. Most often, bush elephants are found in open grasslands, marshes, and lakeshores. They range over most of Africa south of the Sahara Desert.

The other, less numerous subspecies is the forest African elephant (*Loxodonta africana cyclotis*). Compared with the bush elephant, its ears are usually smaller and rounder, and its tusks are also thinner and straighter. The forest elephant can weigh up to ten thousand pounds and stand about ten feet tall. Much less is known about these animals than their bush cousins because environmental and political obstacles make them very difficult to study. Normally they inhabit the dense forests of central and western Africa, though occasionally they do inhabit the edges of forests and overlap territories with their neighbors.

The Asian elephant

As a function of dwindling numbers, it is hard to understand why so much attention is focused on the African elephant's plight when the Asian population is much more threatened than its more popular relative. Today scientists estimate the world population of Asian elephants, or *Elephas maximus*, to be approximately forty thousand, less than one-tenth the number of African elephants. Perhaps the Asian elephant's decline has been less noticeable because it has been more gradual. The causes of this decline are much the same as that of the African.

As with the *Loxodonta*, there are distinct subspecies of *Elephas maximus*. In general, the Asian elephant is smaller than the African. It has smaller ears, shaped like the subcontinent of India, and typically only the males have large external tusks. An Asian elephant can also be distinguished by the large bulges on its forehead, a much hairier body, and various patches of depigmentation (or pink spots) on the skin.

The first subspecies is the Sri Lankan Asian elephant (*Elephas maximus maximus*). Found only on the island of Sri Lanka, a small country off the southeast coast of India, it is the largest of the Asians. According to University of Bombay's J. C. Daniel, there are an estimated total of thirty-five thousand members of this subspecies left today. Large males can weigh upward of twelve thousand pounds and stand over eleven feet tall. Sri Lankan males have very large cranial bulges, and both sexes have more areas of depigmentation than are found in the other Asians. Typically their ears, face, trunk, and belly have large concentrations of pink-speckled skin.

Another subspecies, the mainland Asian elephant (*Elephas maximus indicus*) makes up the bulk of the Asian elephant population. Numbering approximately thirty-six thousand, these elephants are lighter gray in color, with depigmentation only on the ears and trunk. Large males will ordinarily weigh only about eleven thousand pounds but are as tall as the Sri Lankan. The mainland Asian can be found in twelve Asian countries, from India to Indonesia. It prefers forested areas and transitional zones, between forests and grasslands, where greater food variety is available.

The smallest of all the elephants is the Sumatran Asian elephant (*Elephas maximus sumatranus*). Population estimates for this group range from thirty-three hundred to fifty-three hundred individuals. It is very light gray and has less depigmentation than the other Asians, with pink spots only on the ears. Mature Sumatrans will usually only measure about ten feet at the shoulder and weigh less than nine thousand pounds. An enormous animal nonetheless, it is considerably smaller than its other Asian (and African) cousins and exists only on the island of Sumatra, usually in forested regions and partially wooded habitats.

Anatomy

Being mammals, elephants are in some ways biologically similar to humans. They are warm-blooded, have hair on their bodies, nurse their young, and even have a comparable life span, fifty to seventy years. However, their large size and unusual habits have forced them to develop many unique physical adaptations. The special needs of elephants, unfortunately, make them very sensitive to changes in their environment. They need enormous tracts of land to range across, adequate shade, access to large bodies of water, and as diverse a gene pool as possible to keep their population healthy. In adapting to less than ideal environments, elephants have developed anatomical features that have been refined in very interesting ways.

Skin

Another name for an elephant is pachyderm, which means "thick skin." An elephant's skin is extremely tough around most parts of its body. However, the skin around the mouth and inside of the ear is paper thin. Normally, the skin of an Asian is covered with more hair than its African counterpart. This is most noticeable in the young. Asian calves are usually covered with a thick coat of brownish red fuzz. As they get older, this hair darkens and becomes more sparse, but it will always remain on their heads and tails.

Both species of elephants are typically grayish in color, but the Africans very often appear brown or reddish from wallowing in mud holes of colored soil. Wallowing is actually a very important behavior in elephant society. Not only is it important for socialization, but the mud acts as a sunscreen, protecting their skin from harsh ultraviolet radiation. Though tough, an elephant's skin is very sensitive. Without regular mud baths to protect it from burning, as well as from insect bites and moisture loss, an elephant's skin would suffer serious damage. After bathing, the elephant will usually use its trunk to blow dirt on its body to help dry and bake on its new protective coat. As elephants are limited to

smaller and smaller areas, there is less water available, and local herds will often come to blows over the right to use these limited resources.

A zoo elephant throws dirt upon itself as a protection against sun and insects.

Wallowing also aids the skin in regulating body temperature. Elephants spend every day fighting an uphill battle to stay cool. They have a very difficult time releasing heat through the skin because, in proportion to their body size, they have very little of it. The ratio of an elephant's mass to the surface area of its skin is many times that of a human. Elephants have even been observed lifting up their legs to expose the soles of their feet, presumably in an effort to expose more skin to the air. Since wild elephants live in very hot climates, they must have other means of getting rid of excess heat.

Ears

The large flapping ears of an elephant are also very important for temperature regulation. Elephant ears are made of a very thin layer of skin stretched over cartilage and a rich network of blood vessels. On hot days, elephants will flap their ears constantly, creating a slight breeze. This breeze cools the surface blood vessels, and then the cooler blood gets circulated to the rest of the animal's body. The hot blood entering the ears can be cooled as much as ten degrees Fahrenheit before returning to the body. Differences in the ear sizes of African and Asian elephants can be explained, in part, by their geographical distribution. Africans originated and stayed near the equator, where it is warmer. Therefore, they have much bigger ears. Asians live farther north, in slightly cooler climates, and thus have smaller ears.

The ears are also used in certain displays of aggression and during the males' mating period. If an elephant wants to intimidate a predator or rival, it will spread its ears out wide to make itself look more massive and imposing. During the breeding season, males give off an odor from a gland located behind their eyes. Joyce Poole, a well-known elephant researcher, has theorized that the males will fan their ears in an effort to help propel this "elephant cologne" great distances.

Teeth

Elephants' teeth are actually very different from those of most other mammals. Over their lives they have 26 teeth, including 2 upper incisors (tusks), 12 premolars, and 12 molars. Unlike most mammals, which grow baby teeth and then replace them with a permanent set of adult teeth, elephants have cycles of tooth rotation throughout their entire life. After one year the tusks are permanent, but the other teeth are replaced six times in an elephant's life. The teeth don't emerge from the jaws vertically like humans' do with new teeth replacing old ones from above or below. Instead, they have a horizontal progression, like a conveyor belt. New teeth grow in at the back of the mouth, pushing older teeth toward the front, where they become brittle and fall out, making room for more teeth. When an elephant becomes very old, the last set of teeth become brittle, and it must rely on softer foods to chew. Very elderly elephants often spend their final years exclusively in marshy areas, where they can feed on soft wet grasses. Eventually, when the final teeth fall out, the animal will be unable to eat and it will die. However, as more habitat is destroyed, the elephants' living space becomes smaller and smaller; the elderly no longer have the opportunity to roam in search of more appropriate food and will, consequently, die of starvation at an earlier age.

Tusks

The tusks of an elephant are upper incisors that are continuously growing. An adult male's tusks will grow about seven inches a year. Tusks are indispensable to an elephant. They are used primarily to dig for water, salt, and roots; to debark trees, in order to get at the tasty pulp inside; and to move downed trees and branches when clearing a path. In addition, they are used for marking trees to establish territory and occasionally as weapons. Like humans who are typically right- or left-handed, elephants are usually right- or left-tusked. The dominant tusk, called the master tusk, is generally shorter and more rounded at the tip from wear. Both male and female African elephants have large, impressive tusks that can reach over ten feet in length and weigh over two hundred pounds. In the Asian species, only the males have large tusks. Female Asians' tusks are very small or absent altogether. Asian males can have tusks as long as the much larger Africans, but they are usually much slimmer and lighter (the heaviest recorded was only eighty-six pounds). The tusk of both species is mostly made of calcium and phosphate. As a piece of living tissue, it is relatively soft (compared with other minerals such as rock), and the tusk, also known as ivory, is strongly favored by artisans for its carvability. The desire

An elephant's tusks are extremely versatile. Used for digging, obtaining food, and as a weapon, a male's tusks can reach over ten feet.

for elephant ivory has been one of the major factors in the dramatic decline of the world's elephant populations.

Trunk

The proboscis, or trunk, is perhaps the elephant's most distinctive feature. It is a fusion of the nose and upper lip, elongated and specialized to become the elephant's most important and versatile appendage. The trunk is basically used to manipulate objects. To facilitate this, African elephants are equipped with two fingerlike projections at the tip of their trunk, while Asians have only one. According to biologists, the elephant's trunk is said to have over forty thousand individual muscles in it, making it sensitive enough to pick up a single blade of grass, yet strong enough to rip the branches off a tree.

Most herbivores (plant eaters, like the elephant) are adapted with teeth for cutting and tearing off plant materials. However, except for the very young or infirm, elephants always use their trunks to tear up their food and then place it in their mouth. They will graze on grass or reach up into trees to grasp leaves, fruits, or entire branches. If the desired food item is too high up, the elephant will wrap its trunk around the tree or branch and shake its food loose or sometimes simply knock the tree down altogether.

The trunk is also used for drinking. Elephants suck water up into the trunk (up to fifteen quarts at a time) and then blow it into their mouth. Elephants also inhale water to spray on their body during bathing. On top of this watery coating, the animal will then spray dirt and mud, which act as a protective sunscreen.

This amazing appendage also plays a key role in many social interactions. Familiar elephants will greet each other by entwining their trunks, much like a handshake. They also use them while play-wrestling, caressing during courtship, and for dominance displays—a raised trunk can be a warning or threat, while a lowered trunk can be a sign of submission. Elephants can defend themselves very well by flailing their trunk at unwanted intruders or by grasping and flinging them.

An elephant also relies on its trunk for its highly developed sense of smell. Raising the trunk up in the air and swiveling it from side to side, like a periscope, it can determine the location of friends, enemies, and food sources.

Two elephants play in the water, trunks intertwined. Elephants use their trunks almost like hands, including to wrestle and play.

Feeding

A wild elephant will spend most of its life in pursuit of the vast quantities of food it needs to survive. An adult will spend almost twenty hours a day looking for food, and each day will eat between three hundred and six hundred pounds of vegetation. Its astonishing rate of consumption is necessary for two reasons: First, its enormous mass requires a huge amount of food, and second, an elephant's stomach is a very inefficient digestive machine. Many herbivores have several chambered stomachs, allowing them to process their food several times, and, thereby, extracting more nutrients. Elephants have only one chamber, so much

An African elephant consumes native plants. An adult will eat between three and six hundred pounds of vegetation a day.

of the food they eat passes through their body partially or completely undigested. It is this incredible need for food that makes it so difficult to confine elephants to small reserves. They are often very destructive in their feeding habits, knocking down or uprooting entire trees. To find the variety and amount of food they need, they must constantly be on the move. This causes obvious complications when someone builds a farm or house between them and their next food source.

When an animal takes in this much food, it leaves behind an extraordinary amount of waste material. Elephants will defecate up to twenty times a day. Their plentiful wastes are an important part of the ecosystem they occupy. Elephant waste acts as fertilizer for plants and trees, and it is a food source for many insects since much of the waste contains undigested material. One researcher, Leonard Lee Rue, has noted another possible service that elephant waste provides. Rue claims that elephants swallow whole seed pods of the Doum palm tree and pass them out completely undigested. This has no obvious benefit to the elephant, but, apparently, pods that have passed through the elephant's digestive tract sprout better than those that don't. Thus an elephant's feeding patterns are an important link in the web that holds its ecosystem together. By altering where elephants can roam and what they can eat, the ecological structure of a region can be subtly but significantly affected.

Social behavior

Elephants live in a very structured social order. The social lives of male and female elephants are very different. The females spend their entire lives in tightly knit family groups made up of mothers, daughters, sisters, and aunts.

These groups are led by the eldest female, or matriarch. Adult males, on the other hand, live mostly solitary lives.

The social circle of the female elephant doesn't end with the small family unit. In addition to encountering the local males that live on the fringes of one or more groups, the female's life also involves interaction with other families, clans, and subpopulations. Most immediate family groups range from five to fifteen adults, as well as a number of immature males and females. When a group gets too big, a few of the elder daughters will break off and form their own small group. They remain very aware of which local herds are relatives and which are not.

The life of the adult male is very different. As he gets older, he begins to spend more time at the edge of the herd, gradually going off on his own for hours or days at a time. Eventually, days become weeks, and somewhere around the age of fourteen, the mature male, or bull, sets out from

A family of African elephants gathers near shallow water to cool off. Elephants live in packs of five to fifteen adults.

his natal group for good. While males do live primarily solitary lives, they will occasionally form loose associations with other males. These groups are called bachelor herds. The males spend much more time than the females fighting for dominance with each other. Only the most dominant males will be permitted to breed with cycling females. The less dominant ones must wait their turn. It is usually the older bulls, forty to fifty years old, that do most of the breeding. The dominance battles between males can look very fierce, but typically they inflict very little injury. Most of the bouts are in the form of aggressive displays and bluffs. Ordinarily, the smaller, younger, and less confident animal will back off before any real damage can be done. However, during the breeding season, the battles can get extremely aggressive, and the occasional elephant is injured. During this season, known as musth, a bull will fight with almost any other male it encounters, and it will spend most of its time hovering around the female herds, trying to find a receptive mate.

Elephant calves

Elephant social life, in many ways, revolves around breeding and raising of the calves. A female will usually be ready to breed around the age of thirteen, at which time she will seek out the most "fit" male to mate with. The word *fitness*, in an ecological sense, means the animal best suited to survive in its environment and pass on its genes. Females want to breed with the bigger, stronger, and, most importantly, older males. In this way, they are assuring that their offspring will have the best possible chance of survival. But older, mature males are becoming more and more scarce in the wild because they have the largest tusks and are the primary target of poachers. The females' choices are becoming more limited, and, consequently, the gene pool is becoming weakened.

After a twenty-two-month pregnancy, the mother will give birth to a calf that will weigh about 250 pounds and stand over 2½ feet tall. Elephants have a very long childhood. They are born with fewer survival instincts than

many other animals. Instead, they must rely on their elders to teach them the things they need to know. The ability to pass on information and knowledge to their young has always been a major asset in the elephant's struggle to survive. Today, however, the pressures humans have put on the wild elephant populations, from poaching to habitat destruction, mean that the elderly often die at a younger age, leaving fewer teachers for the young.

All members of the tightly knit female group participate in the care and protection of the young. Since everyone in these herds is related, there is never a shortage of babysitters. In fact, a new calf is usually the center of attention for all herd members. All the adults and most of the other young will gather around the newborn, touching and caressing it with their trunks. The baby is born nearly blind and at first relies, almost completely, on its trunk to discover the world around it.

A calf walks with its mother and other female herd members. Babies weigh about 250 pounds when born.

Allomothers

After the initial excitement dies down, the mother will usually select several full-time baby-sitters, or "allomothers," from her group. According to Cynthia Moss, a well-known researcher, these allomothers will help in all aspects of raising the calf. They walk with the young as the herd travels, helping the calves along if they fall or get stuck in the mud. The allomothers will also run to a calf's aid if it makes a distress call, stand over the calves while they sleep, and chase them back to the herd if the calves wander off. The more allomothers a baby has, the more free time its mother has to feed herself. Providing a calf with nutritious milk means the mother has to eat more nutritious food herself. So, the more allomothers, the better the calf's chances of survival.

The elephants' survival, however, also depends on several factors beyond their control. Staying alive in the wild is a difficult task for any animal, but that task has been complicated by the influence of increasing human populations. Today the elephant must battle not only nature and genetics, but also the greed of humans. One of the most significant problems facing the elephant today is the practice of illegal hunting, mostly aimed at gathering tusks to supply the never-ending demand for ivory.

2

The Ivory Trade

MOST SCIENTISTS, CONSERVATIONISTS, and just about anyone who has kept up on current events would agree that the ivory trade has been responsible for decimating a large part of the world's elephant population. However, this industry may yet prove to be the catalyst in saving these endangered species: So much attention has been focused on ivory in recent years that people from all corners of the globe have become acutely aware of the elephant's plight.

Most of the information we hear about the ivory trade revolves around the African elephant. The Asian elephant is also hunted for its tusks, but not to the same extent because its smaller tusks have made it a less cost-effective target. Historically, then, the bulk of the world's ivory has come from Africa.

An ancient industry

The collection and crafting of ivory is by no means a new trade. The practice has been around since the beginning of recorded history. The first ivory carvings on record date back six thousand years to ancient Egypt. Archaeologists have even found carved figurines made from mammoth ivory, which dates back twenty thousand years. It is the unique quality of ivory that has made it very popular. Hard and durable yet easy to carve and fairly flexible, it withstands temperature changes and polishes to a high gloss. Virtually every ancient civilization has left behind evidence of ivory use.

The Egyptians were able to collect elephant tusks from nearby Sudan, and they used them to fashion objects, from decorative figurines to combs and jewelry. In ancient Greece, ivory was a very popular material for sculpting the Greek gods and goddesses. The Romans used it for furnishings and personal adornments. And in medieval Europe and Islamic countries, ivory was fashioned into caskets and boxes, worked with intricate designs. Japan also has a long history of ivory use: In that country, it was made into *netsukes* and *hankos*. *Netsukes* are small toggles or clasps for kimonos, which have been carved in the shape of tiny animals and people. *Hankos* are basically signature stamps made of ivory. Even today both *netsukes* and *hankos* are popular items in Japan. But the most intricate ivory work comes from China. China is famous for its elaborate ivory carvings, exemplified by the marvelously designed "Chinese balls." Two or three concentric balls are carved from a single piece of ivory and worked in minuscule detail. In modern times, ivory has been a favored material throughout the world as inlay for tables, billiard balls, piano keys, statues, and jewelry. While its popularity hasn't changed much over the centuries, the method of collecting the raw material has.

This elephant ivory tusk was carved in southern Italy around 1100. Throughout history, artisans used ivory to carve elaborate works of art.

The hunt

Elephants have been hunted by their local human neighbors for thousands of years. Evidence of the ritualized hunt survives in prehistoric cave drawings and Persian tapestries. Much about the hunt, however, has changed in the last couple centuries. Ancient tribes utilized methods passed down by their ancestors for many generations. Some recorded methods included enormous pit traps; sneaking up to the animal and cutting off the trunk so it would bleed to death; or slicing the back of the legs, just above the heel, to incapacitate the animal until it was separated from the herd. These methods may appear harsh by today's standards, but elephants can be a deadly foe; without the modern convenience of firearms, tracking devices, and motor vehicles, the hunters had to be willing to use any means necessary to capture their prey.

After the slaughter, the meat, fat, and ivory were distributed among the members of the tribe according to their status and participation in the hunt (the one responsible for the lethal blow always received the largest portion). This method of hunting only what they needed kept the local tribes of Africa and Asia well fed and the elephant populations well maintained. Things changed dramatically, though, after European colonization of Africa and Asia in the nineteenth century. Since that time, the killing of elephants has increased more than a hundredfold, due primarily to the rise of sport hunting and the use of firearms. No longer was the elephant killed to sustain one tribe for days or even weeks. Now, through the use of sophisticated weaponry, thousands were being slaughtered for sport and to have their meat and ivory shipped out all over the world.

The beginning of the end

Ivory has been a universally and consistently valuable commodity. However, historically the ivory trade has been cyclical. According to Roger DiSilvestro, author of *The African Elephant*, there have been two great explosions in the ivory trade. The first occurred during the Roman Empire.

During the first century A.D., Romans used an extraordinary amount of ivory, causing a severe shortage. The Romans continued to trade on a grand scale and were responsible, in large part, for the permanent disappearance of the elephant from northern Africa, around the seventh century. At that time Rome turned to Ethiopia and Somalia for new supplies.

The second great boom in the ivory trade occurred in the nineteenth century, mainly for two reasons, according to DiSilvestro. First, the Industrial Revolution brought sudden wealth to many Europeans and Americans, who displayed their affluence in material luxuries, including ivory buttons, brush handles, letter openers, figurines, fans, and similar fancies. The second factor was the creation of well-established trade routes by Arab merchants. Modern trade began with Sa'id ibn Sultan, the collective ruler of all of Africa's Arab settlements. In 1840 he established his base in Zanzibar (now Tanzania) and made it the commercial capital of the western Indian Ocean. Ivory was high on the list of trade items and forced Sa'id deep into Africa to supply the demands of his customers.

Early attempts to control ivory trade

During most of the 1800s, Britain controlled eastern Africa and its hugely profitable ivory trade. A worldwide ban on the sale of ivory was almost a century away, but, even then, attempts were made to manage and control the trade. Most of these nineteenth-century laws were very poorly enforced and basically ignored until 1910, when national preserves were set up to provide the elephants with a protected area. Poaching continued even after the establishment of these preserves. In fact, during this time, illegal poaching by local people went up considerably. Many natives resented being displaced by the creation of the new parks, as well as being told that they could no longer hunt elephants at will, as their ancestors had done for generations. Therefore, they were vulnerable to the poachers' lures of money, alcohol, firearms, and drugs. The elephant's decline accelerated as the decades passed.

During a two-year period in the 1950s in Kenya's Tsavo National Park, natives killed seven thousand elephants. Hunting them as their ancestors had, they might not have killed that many in two centuries.

After the fall of colonial governments during the 1960s and 1970s, the ivory trade escalated as newly independent African states struggled to establish stable economies and governments. Poaching control was simply not a priority, and corruption was widespread. For example, the biggest dealer in illegal ivory was Kenya's United African Corporation. The company was run by Margaret Kenyatta, who happened to be the mayor of Nairobi and the daughter of the Kenyan president. The price of raw ivory rose from $2.50 a pound in the late 1960s, to $50 a pound in 1978, and reached a high of $114 a pound in the Orient during the 1980s. Local poachers actually received only a tiny fraction of this money, but in terms of average income in

Elephant tusks are arranged in preparation for an auction in 1977. It is startling to remember that every pair of tusks represents a dead elephant.

the region, the death of just two elephants and the resulting sale of their ivory earned a poacher an entire year's wage.

Deaths reached an all-time high in the 1980s. By then, mature males, with the largest tusks, had been nearly wiped out, so poachers were forced to kill larger numbers of smaller, younger elephants to gather the same amount of ivory. During the 1980s, Kenya lost 85 percent of its elephants, and Tanzania lost 22,000 a year. In 1976 Tanzania's Selous Game Reserve contained 109,000 elephants, reduced by the end of the 1980s to 30,000. Chad's 15,000 elephants were reduced to 2,000 during the same period. An aerial survey of Somalia during the late 1980s counted more dead elephants than living ones. Another frightening discovery was made around Tanzania's Lake Manyara: In 1969 there were 125 matriarchs, or older herd leaders; by 1989, only three were left alive. This meant that the inexperienced teenage females were left to run the herds, a job they normally would not take on for another twenty or thirty years. Without the extended knowledge of terrain and water sources, they were in no position to lead these groups. By this time, it was becoming obvious that something needed to be done. In fact, the wheels had already been put in motion for stricter laws governing elephant poaching.

The ivory ban

In October 1989 over one hundred nations joined together to ban ivory from the world market. This extremely controversial decision was the culmination of a fifteen-year intensive study of the African elephant's population. This study involved many different organizations but was headquartered and coordinated in Nairobi, Kenya, under the direction of the United Nations Environment Programme (UNEP). In 1976 the International Union for the Conservation of Nature (IUCN) was supported by the World Wildlife Fund (WWF) and the New York Zoological Society (NYZS) in creating the Elephant Survey and Conservation Program. This group carried out research on certain critical elephant populations in an effort to determine the range, status, and population trends of the species. This was done through the review of previous research and literature, distributing questionnaires, and bringing together a large number of elephant experts from around the world.

The worldwide treaty responsible for governing all animal trade is called CITES (Convention on the International Trade in Endangered Species). This conservation treaty has more than 115 signatories, or participating countries. When a country joins CITES, it agrees to control or prohibit trade in live or dead specimens (or parts) of endangered species that are assigned one of three classifications: Appendix I (no commercial trade at all), Appendix II (controlled trade), or Appendix III (monitored trade). The Asian elephant has been listed on Appendix I since the inception of CITES in 1976 since there are less than fifty thousand left in the world. However, the African population, estimated at close to 2 million in 1976, was not listed on Appendix II until 1977.

In 1979 preliminary results of the IUCN study indicated a population of approximately 1.3 million African elephants. According to the research, this was a significant decline in the overall *Loxodonta* population, and the ivory trade was recognized as a major factor. However, certain populations were locally overabundant. In other words, while most African countries showed huge losses in elephants, some countries actually had too many. The local governments of these countries claimed that they had to "cull," or kill off, some elephants each year in order to keep their numbers from rising out of control. As a result of these inconclusive findings, the African elephant remained on Appendix II that year.

Lack of enforcement

In 1985 CITES attempted a compromise by setting up an ivory control system designed to tighten international trade restrictions on ivory. Quotas were set, and legally collected ivory was supposed to be tagged and numbered before shipping. The problem with this was that CITES had no enforcement capabilities. Each signatory is supposed to take on the responsibility of imposing laws and

Members of an anti-poaching unit relax around a campfire. Although such poaching units have been successful in capturing some poachers, their numbers are usually too few to be able to make a significant dent in the amount of poaching.

consequences for poaching and illegal trade in its own country. Trade permits were easily forged, and some countries were corrupt in the distribution of these permits. In addition, any signatory can enter a reservation about a specific CITES ruling, basically saying that they don't agree with it and won't abide by it. Burundi was well known for its abuse of these regulations. In a thirteen-year period, it exported over two thousand tons of ivory, even though Burundi has no native elephant population. Presumably, the Burundi government confiscated illegally obtained ivory from smugglers passing through and then sold it. This kind of illegal laundering scheme was not uncommon, and the lack of effective enforcement continued to be a large problem. Often poachers were much better armed and equipped than the rangers. During the late 1980s, poachers in Kenya used automatic assault rifles against rangers armed with old World War II rifles.

The ban left many governments and private businesses with warehouses full of stockpiled ivory, which they could no longer sell legally. On several occasions, CITES authorized the legal sale of hundreds of tons of ivory stockpiles, in hopes that this would flush the existing supply of ivory out of the market. In 1986 one warehouse in Singapore that had amassed three hundred tons of ivory was given permission to sell it off without recrimination. In most cases, these efforts did empty the warehouses, but not for long—the now wealthy owners and poachers simply refilled them with illegally obtained ivory. In addition, between 1985 and 1989 approximately two-thirds of CITES's ivory control system budget came from donations made by ivory traders. This obvious conflict of interest raised many questions about some of the decisions that were being made. Conservation groups were beginning to realize that the current efforts were simply not working.

The great ivory debate

Many opponents of the ban claimed that the research presented in 1979 was unreliable. So efforts were made to improve the data. From 1986 on, all elephant reporting was funneled through the African Elephant and Rhino Specialist Group (AERSG). Created by the IUCN, this new group was comprised of scientists from different parts of Africa. The AERSG went over all research, determined its validity, and questioned any unclear findings. All cleared research was then entered into the UNEP computer system.

In 1987 AERSG determined, through its refined and presumably more accurate research, that the total African elephant population was now down to 760,000. For the first time, all scientists involved agreed that ivory trade was a major factor in the decline and that the overall elephant population would soon be endangered. But despite these efforts, the African elephant remained on Appendix II. The southern African countries still maintained that their elephant populations were stable or rising, and collectively they remained opponents of an outright ivory ban.

The next CITES conference was scheduled for late 1989. Supporters and opponents of a ban spent the two-year interval preparing for what was sure to be a very heated debate. The AERSG commissioned a group of biologists, population modelers, economists, lawyers, and journalists—known collectively as the Ivory Trade Review Group—to analyze the specific effects of the ivory trade on the African elephant. In 1988 the African Wildlife Foundation, based in

Washington, D.C., began an all-out campaign to end the ivory trade. They attempted to raise the public's awareness of the elephant's current situation. In response to these efforts, the U.S. Congress enacted the African Elephant Conservation Act, prohibiting the import of any ivory that does not strictly adhere to CITES regulations. The next year both the United States and Japan imposed a complete ban on all raw and worked ivory products.

In October 1989 elephants were at the top of the CITES agenda. The latest and most reliable research presented at the convention indicated that the overall African elephant population was now down to 609,000. Compared with reports just ten years earlier of 1.3 million individuals, this drop was staggering. Regional surveys concluded that in these ten years eastern Africa had lost 74 percent of its elephants; central Africa over 80 percent; and southern Africa's elephant population had remained stable, with the country of South Africa actually seeing a 5 percent increase each year.

A vital source of income

Many southern African countries, including Zimbabwe, Zambia, South Africa, Botswana, Malawi, and Namibia, were still opposed to the ban and presented arguments against it. They claimed they had been very diligent and successful in managing their elephant populations. As a result, they have an overpopulation in their limited preserves and need to cull elephants each year to keep the rest from starving to death. They felt that the sale of ivory from these legally culled elephants was a vital part of their countries' incomes, and a complete ivory ban would unfairly deprive them of this. Money raised from the sale of ivory, hides, and meat helps to pay for schools, clinics, and the conservation of elephants and other animals in protected areas. They also argued that local people only tolerate the crop damage caused by elephants every year because they know the animals have a cash value to their government. According to Henri Nsanjama of Malawi's wildlife department, "[Without a price on their heads], they will kill them just to get rid of

"IT'S REALLY BETTER THIS WAY. AT THE MOST, I'LL GET MUGGED."

them. The elephant becomes a giant pest." Furthermore, these countries argued, making ivory completely illegal will force the market underground, where it could not be monitored at all. As an example, they cited the recent ban on rhino horn. Shortly after that ban, rhino horn prices went through the roof, which provided added incentive to the poachers and resulted in a massacre of the African rhino population. The coalition suggested, as an alternative to the ban, that central and eastern African countries should send officials to southern Africa to learn from them how to better manage their elephant herds and keep poaching down.

The advocates of the ban argued that only a complete elimination of all ivory trade would save the species. Any legal trade at all leaves the door open somewhere for illegal ivory to be laundered into the market. They also claimed that there was, in reality, very little economic gain for the individual governments involved in legal ivory trade. Only a small percentage of the retail sale, no more than a few hundred thousand dollars a year, actually reached the national treasuries. Ecotourism, on the other hand, brought in over $500 million a year in Kenya alone. The elephants are a very large part of this tourism industry. In fact, a survey of safari operators and tourists in Kenya estimated that the elephants alone bring in about $200 million a year. So, according to the ban advocates, the elephants actually have a higher cash value alive than dead.

The central and eastern African representatives also argued that a ban on ivory trade should have no effect on countries forced to cull elephants, if the culling is truly necessary for ecological reasons, as opponents claim, and not financial ones. Besides, they maintained, most of the revenue derived from dead elephants in southern Africa came from the sale of sport hunting licenses, not ivory sales (CITES does not prohibit a hunter from taking home his own trophies). They also dismissed the invitation to adopt the more successful poacher management methods used in the southern countries. They explained that these methods are effective but very costly. Unlike the wealthier nations of South Africa and Zimbabwe, the poverty-stricken nations of central and eastern Africa could never afford to put these methods into practice. Finally, they pointed out the trends revealed by the newest research, which indicated that poachers typically decimated one area completely and then moved on to new, untouched territory. It can be assumed, they said, that when all the elephants have been eliminated from eastern and central Africa, the poachers will move on to the better-protected areas of the south.

The verdict

After hearing all the arguments, the signatories voted. It was decided that the African elephant would be moved to Appendix I, effectively outlawing all international trade in elephant parts. As expected, most of the southern African countries voted against the ban, including Zimbabwe, Zambia, South Africa, Mozambique, Gabon, Burundi, Botswana, Cameroon, and Congo. The only non-African nations that voted against the ban were Argentina and China. Six countries (China, Zimbabwe, Zambia, Botswana, South Africa, and Mozambique) entered reservations against the ban—as was their right under CITES—stating that they did not agree with it and would not participate in it.

The WWF conducted a survey in 1990 to determine the impact of the ban, and the results were clear. The demand for ivory had virtually dried up. Sales had dropped off in most industrialized countries by 40 to 70 percent. By the end of 1990 most Chinese and Hong Kong ivory-carving factories had laid off the majority of their staff or shut down completely. The effect on African elephant populations was also quite dramatic. For example, Tsavo National Park, in Kenya, had reported 160 elephant carcasses due to poaching in 1988. In 1991 not one carcass was found. Fears about the ban causing prices to skyrocket proved to be unfounded. According to Jorgen Thomson of TRAF-FIC, an international trade monitoring organization, ivory that was selling for $50 to $70 a kilo in Somalia is now going for $5 to $10.

A new attitude

Today efforts to protect the elephant have become a priority in both the industrialized and Third World nations,

Carved elephant tusks sit in a Hong Kong ivory shop. Hong Kong was one of the biggest buyers of ivory.

largely due to the 1989 CITES decision. However, the real turning point in world opinion may have occurred three months earlier in Nairobi, Kenya. On July 17 of that year, Kenya's president, Daniel arap Moi, made the world take notice when he publicly burned over thirteen tons of stockpiled ivory tusks valued at roughly $3 million. Like most African nations, Kenya had stored all the ivory it confiscated from poachers and traders, in the hope of someday selling it through legal channels and thus providing its citizens with desperately needed income. President Moi's public destruction of his nation's stockpile was a symbolic gesture, emphasizing Kenya's determination to halt the illegal slaughter of its elephants. According to Richard Leakey, at that time in charge of Kenya's wildlife management, it was necessary to get the attention of consumers, who are used to being influenced by advertising campaigns. "We were determined to demonstrate our commitment. We felt it hypocritical to say 'Don't buy ivory' to the world while we were selling it. So . . . we burned ivory and the world noticed!"

Richard Leakey poses with some of the twelve tons of poached ivory tusks that will be burned. Leakey was one of the first to appeal directly to consumers in the fight against illegal ivory products.

Progress in Kenya

After 1989 efforts at poaching control and ivory trade regulation were increased dramatically. Appointed to head up Kenya's Wildlife Services, Leakey completely restructured the department. In just a few years, he managed to eliminate corrupt officials and rangers, raise considerable funds, and increase the rangers' job training. By soliciting donations and convincing the Kenyan government to grant his department a share of the nation's tourism proceeds, he was able to provide rangers with automatic weapons, uniforms, and communications equipment and to double their salaries. All rangers are now required to complete nine months of paramilitary

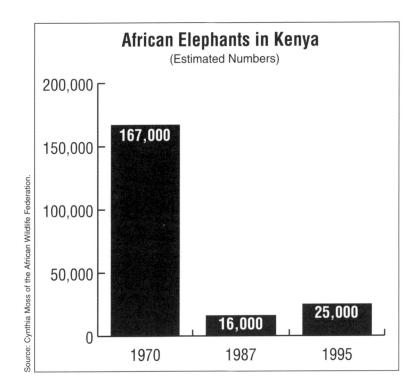

training and a year of wildlife management study. In the first fourteen months of Leakey's administration, seventy-five poachers were killed. Poaching in Kenya came nearly to a halt. Not all countries can compare their records to Kenya's, but similar trends can be seen throughout the region. Of course, the battle is hardly over; some nations are still unhappy about the trade restrictions and continue to seek a change.

The controversy continues

As elephant populations stabilize, several southern African countries claim that they need to continue culling their herds and want to reinstate a legal ivory trade. Zimbabwe, Zambia, Botswana, Malawi, and Namibia have joined together to form the Southern Africa Center for Ivory Marketing (SACIM). This group has petitioned at each subsequent CITES conference to return the African elephant back to Appendix II and loosen controls over ivory trade. Most of the countries agree that the renewal of any ivory trade will stimulate the illegal poaching and trade once again. The SACIM argues that new methods of tracing a tusk's origin make it feasible to differentiate between legally and illegally obtained ivory.

In fact, new forensic methods are being refined to make such a distinction possible, but they are not yet perfected. For example, DNA testing of the soft muscle tissue attached to the base of an elephant's trunk can be used to identify a DNA "fingerprint" unique to each animal. Once different herds throughout Africa are DNA-typed, these fingerprints can then help to trace a tusk's origin.

Another possibility concerns the mineral composition of the tusk itself. Elephants are strictly plant eaters, and the availability and distribution of local plant materials in certain African regions cause unique chemical traces to be deposited in the tusks as they grow. By studying the exact diets of specific elephant herds, scientists are now coming up with a key for a kind of chemical code found in the tusks. These new methods may allow law enforcement agencies to determine if ivory came from legal cullings in southern Africa or illegal poaching in central or eastern Africa. Whether or not the *Loxodonta* are returned to Appendix II, these new techniques will help to further crack down on illegal trade. However, the elephant's survival depends on much more than just the sale of its ivory. Humans encroach into its territory more and more each year; unless the elephant is permitted a stable place to live, it will be lost to poachers and tourists alike.

3

Habitat Loss

THE THREAT TO the elephant presented by the ivory trade is unique to the species. However, the second critical, and perhaps more complicated, threat to the elephant's survival is one affecting wildlife throughout the planet. The earth is a living biomass and can support only a limited amount of life. As one species increases, typically another must give way somewhere in the world. The human species has expanded at a rate unprecedented in the history of our planet. According to a Global 2000 Report, by the turn of the century, there will be about 6 billion people on the planet. As a result of this human expansion, an equally unprecedented number of plant and animal species are losing their habitats and disappearing.

As the most successful animal species, adapted to just about any environment, humans compete with other animals for space and resources. Humans' increased intelligence also gave them the foresight to realize in modern times that many neighboring species were on their way toward extinction. Some people began to take measures in an effort to slow this trend. One of the most effective ways to give other species a fighting chance is to preserve and protect large tracts of undeveloped land.

National parks

The IUCN recognizes several categories of protected land. A reserve is an area of land set aside by any local district, corporation, or even an individual. Since this land can be privately owned and controlled, its status can be overturned very easily. A national park on the other hand, can only be established by the highest authority in the nation, usually by legislation, and is much harder to override. To date, no national park in the world has ever been deproclaimed (though some have been reduced in size).

Africa's first official reserve eventually became one of the world's most famous and successful national parks. Kruger National Park in South Africa first became a reserve in the face of great opposition in 1898 (then Sabi Reserve). It was deproclaimed and reproclaimed several times before it was renamed and granted national park status in 1926. It was to be the first of many.

Of course, there were many problems in establishing these reserves. For example, elephants range through a wide tract of land with little regard for national borders. However, when most parks were created, the boundaries were drawn at the man-made borders of individual countries. Once a fence was erected, many animals found themselves cut off from their winter feeding grounds or spring breeding areas. Some animals died as a result, while some, like the elephants, just trampled through the fences. This did little to belie their image as a crop-raiding pest. The more often an elephant wandered off its reserve, the more trouble it got into, and the more chance it had of being shot by an angry farmer. When confined to small territories, elephants can inflict an enormous amount of damage to the local landscapes. Today there are still many problems associated with these parks and reserves, but there is now little question as to whether or not they are necessary. As scientists learn more about nature and the environment, it becomes very clear that these parks may be the elephant's last hope against the rapidly changing world around them.

Deforestation

For hundreds, if not thousands, of years, local people have used a method of farming known as "slash and burn." An area of forest is simply burned to the ground so that its ashes provide fertilizer, enriching the soil for planting crops. After a few seasons, however, the soil is leached of

Kruger National Park

Zimbabwe

Luvuvhu

Limpopo

Mozambique

South
Africa

Olifants

Motswari •

Thornybush •

Mala Mala
Londolozi • •
Sabi Sabi •

Sabie

Park reserve area

its nutrients and is of poor quality for growing anything. At this point, farmers move on to burn down another tract of land, leaving the original spot to replenish itself over the years. When the earth's human population was smaller, this method worked well. Left untouched, the abandoned fields would once again become overgrown with forest life. The original farmers' descendants would then cycle back through these patches of forest in the years to come.

With population growth comes increased demand for land. The cycle between clearing and regrowth becomes shorter and shorter. During the twentieth century, the human population has increased to such a point that plots of land must be reused when nothing but short grass has had a chance to return. Obviously, the soil in these burned fields is not very rich and is useful for an even shorter

The effects of slash-and-burn agriculture can be seen in this forest located in the Himalayan foothills in India.

amount of time, causing farmers to move on to new territory at an alarming rate.

In the last few years, deforestation has been an even bigger problem with increased demands for timber. Worldwide, huge areas of forest are being cleared for the cash value of their trees. Many of the native trees that are felled take hundreds of years to regrow, so reforestation plans often involve the planting of fast-growth trees, like pine and eucalyptus. These trees will fill in the area quickly, but they are not native species and will not usually support any indigenous wildlife. Zoologists J. and K. MacKinnon refer to these new forests as "zoological deserts" because they are nearly barren of all life.

As larger patches of forest disappear, the ecosystem is affected in profound ways. The trees are responsible for anchoring soil and absorbing water runoff. Floods and massive erosion are common results of deforestation. Elephants need massive tracts of land because, much like the slash-and-burn farmers, they are used to crashing through the forest, tearing down trees and shrubs for food and then cycling back later on, when the area has regrown. As forests are reduced to small pockets, elephants become part of the problem, quickly destroying all the vegetation in an area, eliminating all their resources. This process, unfortunately, can be irreversible and always has long-term consequences.

Overgrazing

Meeting the agricultural demands of an ever-increasing Third World population takes its toll on the land in more ways than one. Overgrazing has caused severe land degradation in Africa and Asia. As more cattle and livestock farms appear in these areas, larger and larger stretches of pasture are needed to feed them. After an area has been overgrazed by cattle, it can still support sheep. After it has become too poor to support sheep, goats can still survive on it. Goats will eat just about anything and are often seen as a practical way to utilize poor-quality, overgrazed land. Unfortunately, goats strip the land to the bone, consuming any vegetation, including shrubs and trees, right down to the bark. What's left behind is of no use to an army of ants, much less a herd of elephants.

Overhunting

Humankind is the only species capable of overhunting another species into extinction. Most carnivorous animals' survival is limited by the number of prey animals available. As prey items begin to decrease, many local predators go hungry and their numbers will thin out as well. Living in this constant state of checks and balances, many species of wild animals have survived for hundreds of thousands of years. If humans' prey dies off, on the other hand, they can move on to alternate animals or simply supplement their omnivorous diets with less protein and more vegetation. As the human species seeks to control its environment, it continues to overhunt across nearly every landscape in the world.

The larger, long-lived, slow-breeding animals, like the elephant, are most susceptible to this overhunting. They cannot hide, and it takes many years for an elephant to grow and reproduce. Also, as other smaller species (including trees and plants) are overharvested, the ecosystem is severely disturbed. The repercussions of this flow up and down the food chain. Again, the elephant usually suffers severely from the situation. An elephant needs an average of three hundred pounds of vegetation a day to survive. As large predators are hunted, the local small grazer populations (the elephant's food competitors) find themselves on the rise. The increased number of herbivores ravage the local trees, shrubs, and grasses. Elephants cannot survive on what remains.

Asia's dwindling habitat

Lacking the massive tusks of its African cousins, the Asian elephant's demise can be attributed mostly to loss of its habitat. J. C. Daniel, researcher and head of Bombay's National History Society, says, "Loss of its habitat is the crux of the problem of the elephant's declining numbers, its endangered status, and threats to its survival." Elephants are found in many parts of Asia, but they are perhaps most commonly associated with the subcontinent of India.

In 1947, when India became an independent nation, its population was approximately 500 million. The same land-mass now supports almost a billion people. At the turn of the twentieth century, it is estimated that about 40 percent

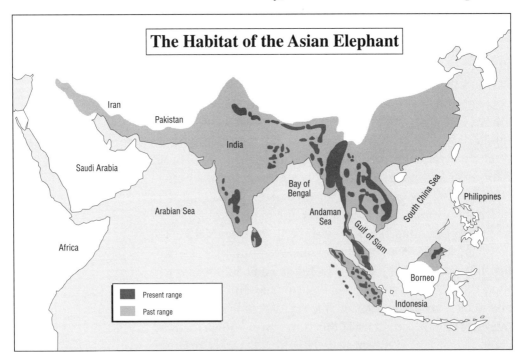

The Habitat of the Asian Elephant

of the country was covered in forest. Today, due to clear-cutting for commercial planting, as well as overgrazing by limitless livestock, the forest remains over only 15 percent of the land. Approximately one-third of this remaining forest has been set aside as wildlife preserves.

Like most developing nations, India has very severe domestic concerns and a lack of funds with which to deal with these problems. There has been much heated debate over whether or not the nation's limited resources should be put toward habitat protection when many of its human inhabitants do not have sufficient food or even running water. As in most countries, the war to save the elephant is fought, to a large extent, by politicians. India's wildlife is afforded as much protection as its government can afford, but each year there are proposals to reduce the amount spent on conservation. Fortunately for wildlife, conservation still has many staunch supporters. Ullas Karanth, outspoken preservationist and researcher of Indian wildlife, is of the opinion that "97% of this country is earmarked for people. On [the other] 3% there must be no compromise. . . . It is primarily a policing job." Voices like Karanth's have made headway: Thirty years ago there were 80 national parks in India. Today there are over 450 and more on the way. Of course, a serious lack of funds means that many of these parks are protected on paper only. Without money for rangers and equipment, patrols for these areas are sadly lacking. Once set aside as a reserve, the success of the parks depends on cooperation from many different levels. Local people have to be willing to relocate or stop poaching and overgrazing the preserves. The government then has to be willing to pay for these relocations and farmer subsidies.

Sri Lanka

Sri Lanka, formerly Ceylon, the island nation off the southeast coast of India, was at one time home to more than twelve thousand elephants. They were an important part of the culture—used as war mounts, captured and exported, and used in private herds as work animals. In the early nineteenth century, as a British colony, Ceylon was the site of massive coffee plantations. As the plantations increased, elephants became a significant pest and bounties were placed on their heads. Elephants were slaughtered by the thousands. One man during the mid–nineteenth century was reported to have killed over thirteen hundred himself. By 1891 people began to be concerned about dwindling elephant populations, and laws were passed to stop the uncontrolled hunting. Pressures on crops from the elephants then increased again, so hunting still continued to a certain extent. According to the IUCN's specialist groups, there are just over three thousand wild elephants left in Sri Lanka today. These elephants all live in one of three national parks: Ruhunu, Wilpattu, and Gal Oya. These parks offer less than guaranteed protection. For example, Ruhunu and Gal Oya are in areas that have a severe dry season. The elephants cannot find food and water during these times, so they migrate to nearby wetlands. These elephants have been making this seasonal migration for centuries, as is evidenced by the existence of very old trails that they still follow. Today, however, the wetlands are crowded with tea and coffee plantations, which the elephants see as a tasty buffet. Compounding the problem is the fact that plantations now exist all along the route they use to reach the wetlands. So, of course, the elephants eat and do more crop damage all along the migration route. People depend on these cash crops for their livelihood, and there are laws to protect humans as well as elephants. Farmers in these areas are legally permitted to shoot elephants who endanger their crops and settlements.

Southeast Asia

Southeast Asia is home to many isolated elephant populations. Unfortunately, many countries in this part of the world are undergoing extreme political upheaval and do not allow Western researchers in very often. One man, Robert Olivier, has been able to penetrate the political and natural blockades of these areas on several occasions. Olivier's research into Myanmar (formerly Burma) showed no officially protected nature preserves at all but lots of remaining forest habitat. In fact, he estimated that there are 149,000 square miles of intact forest in this country. His estimate of the number of elephants in Myanmar remains at about five thousand.

In Thailand, elephants have been protected for centuries, at least in theory if not always in practice. The forests of Thailand once covered 80 percent of the country. Today less than 30 percent of the region is forested, and remaining forest is reduced by 13 percent each year. The elephants of Thailand have been used for many years as domestic animals for agriculture and for war. In 1884 there were reportedly 20,000 domesticated elephants throughout the country. The encroachment of expanding human populations has taken its toll through habitat loss, poaching, and political upheaval. In 1950 there were only 14,000 domesticated elephants there, and today the estimate is between 2,500 and 4,000 individuals.

All island elephants are considered more seriously threatened than their mainland neighbors. They are isolated and have only a limited amount of space to migrate

Baby elephants feast on pineapples, bananas, and sugar cane at the Elephant Conservation Center in Thailand. The feast is a traditional one, organized to honor the elephants.

away from human pressures. They cannot depend on immigration to restock their gene pool, and they are more susceptible to the rapid spread of disease. There is currently some debate as to whether elephants were ever indigenous to the island of Borneo. The ones that remain today seem to have descended from an imported domestic stock, once belonging to the sultan of Sulu in 1750. Estimates of the Bornean population are sketchy at best. The most recent accurate survey, which was conducted in 1968, put their numbers at about two thousand. The neighboring island of Sumatra fares no better. This country does have a few wildlife reserves, but they are very poorly policed. The laws are not enforced, and hunting licenses are easily obtained from local officials. In addition, the populations within the island are extremely fragmented. In 1929 there were up to three thousand elephants in Sumatra; the latest estimates report about three hundred individuals.

The Malayan Elephant

Records indicate that one thousand years ago, the country of Malaya was one of the strongholds of the Asian elephant population. Thriving trade in both ivory and live domesticated elephants occurred between Malaya and other countries. The elephants were revered in this country and were well cared for. At the beginning of the twentieth century, however, Malaya's ancient traditional economy was transformed by the rubber industry. For about thirty years, Malaya's forests were torn down and replanted with rubber trees. This became a big-money industry for the Malayans, and the elephant, having turned to the rubber trees for food, became a major problem. The result, as in many other places throughout the world, was large-scale eradication. Elephants were said to have caused about $30,000 worth of damage to the rubber trees between 1910 and 1930 (a king's ransom to an impoverished nation at the turn of the century).

The elephants ended up retreating to isolated pockets of forest in the eastern part of the peninsula. A new chief game warden in Malaya, Mohammed Khan bin Momin Khan, took up the cause of protecting the herds in 1970.

Their numbers had been so significantly reduced that his efforts, while valiant, may not be enough to save the Malayan elephant. Estimates today are, again, unreliable at best. Two separate studies were carried out in the 1970s: one reported 556 elephants; the other study estimated between 3,000 and 6,000. There are still many Southeast Asian countries isolated from Western research, including Vietnam, Laos, and Cambodia. It may be years before new studies are permitted.

Eastern Africa

Eastern and central Africa have had perhaps the most turbulent recent history with regard to their elephant populations. Most of the countries in this region are poor in comparison with the countries of southern Africa. They have very limited resources, and their citizens are perennially faced with starvation and disease. The lack of funds in these areas has also made them the prime target of ivory poachers. During the last two decades, poachers decimated the local elephant populations. Today, thanks to the CITES ban and increased efforts on the part of several local governments, poaching has nearly come to a standstill. It will, however, take many generations for the elephants of this region to reestablish their numbers. In light of the current African population growth, this may never happen. According to a newsletter put out by the WWF, when Africa had 10 million elephants, there were only 16 million people there. Today Africa's human population is over 500 million, and elephant range has been reduced to less than one-quarter of the continent's surface. Kenya, for example, has an average human growth rate of 4 percent every year. This trend shows no signs of slowing and will obviously mean less territory for the elephant, as well as all of Africa's other wild animals.

One of the more well known reserves in the region is Kenya's Tsavo National Park. In the 1950s, shortly after Tsavo had been established, there were reports of severe damage to its baobab trees. The elephants were ripping off the bark to get at the fleshy interior of the trunk. The new

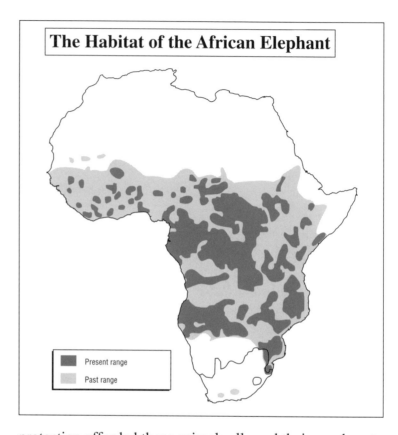

The Habitat of the African Elephant

Present range

Past range

protection afforded these animals allowed their numbers to climb, perhaps too fast. In 1957 the elephant population was estimated at 3,000. Just nine years later, in 1966, an aerial survey reported about 15,000 individuals. Some researchers believe that the 1957 count was in error. However, by 1969 there were 20,000 elephants. The population was swelling well beyond the capacity of the park. The elephants could not leave the grounds because they would be shot by farmers or poached. The inflated population took its toll on Tsavo. Forested areas were being systematically destroyed or reduced to grassland. A new and radical approach was suggested by some: Perhaps the elephants should be culled. Controlled killing to reduce their numbers was not a popular option. Opponents said that this would only be a short-term solution, and there was evidence showing that somehow the elephants were beginning to regulate themselves to some extent. Females were not reaching reproductive maturity until a later age than normal. Some scientists suggested that this could have been due to nutritional deficiencies or hormonal imbalances caused by overcrowding. In 1969 researcher Richard Laws presented the report of the Tsavo Research Project, in which he stated that culling would be necessary to ensure the park's survival. A long and heated debate ensued, but eventually the government decided against culling, in hopes that the elephants would continue to regulate their own numbers. This turned out to be a very fortunate decision. In 1970–1971 there was a devastating drought in the area. Over six thousand elephants died. If culling had also taken place a year or two earlier, the local elephant population might have been too decimated to recover.

Western Africa

Less is known about the elephant population in western Africa than in any other part of the country. Dense, nearly impenetrable forests and unstable political situations have kept most researchers from getting a handle on the forest elephant's current situation. One of the few countries that

A baby elephant nuzzles against its mother in Tsavo National Park in Kenya. Because of Africa's terrain, an accurate count of the elephant population is difficult.

has been studied is Gabon. During the early 1980s, there was a large amount of ivory coming out of the forests of Gabon. This could either mean that the elephant population was being reduced to small numbers or that there was a large sustainable healthy population.

Richard and Karen Barnes found the political climate of Gabon to be fairly stable and consequently were able to conduct detailed research in the area. In the rain forest, it is impossible to count elephants from a jeep or a plane, the way it's done on the savannas. Instead, the Barneses had to rely on taking inventory of droppings and correlating this to approximate herd sizes. What they discovered was actually very encouraging. Seventy-six percent of Gabon is still covered by rain forest. The human population in this country is only a little over 1 million. Rural farmers typically live on the outskirts of the forest, along major roads. The forest elephant is more wary of human contact than its savanna cousins and consequently stays away from these major roads. Decreased contact means decreased friction between humans and elephants. Also, the recent discovery of oil off the coast of Gabon has lured large numbers of rural farmers away from the forest to seek out high-paying jobs in coastal cities. Not only does this cause less human conflict in the area, but increased revenue from the oil industry has taken the pressure off forest exploitation, such as timber and mineral extraction.

The Barneses' most recent data indicate there may be more than seventy thousand wild elephants in Gabon alone. Unfortunately, the rest of equatorial Africa's forest elephant population may not be faring as well. Studies in Zaire and other neighboring countries have shown that teams of organized ivory poachers using automatic weapons have still been operating in the deepest regions of the forest, even since the ban in 1989.

Southern Africa

The countries of southern Africa have traditionally been wealthier than their northern neighbors. As a result, most of these countries have a well-designed, well-equipped, and well-patrolled system of national parks. Perhaps the most successful and frequently visited park in Africa, Kruger National Park, is still growing. Located in the northeast corner of South Africa, Kruger is an enormous park. According to Chief of Tourism Piet du Plessis, it is about 230 miles long and 35 to 40 miles wide along most of its length.

But as vast as it is, even Kruger National Park is only a fraction of its inhabitants' former range. As in any other part of the world, elephants confined to small areas can do major damage. Well-known journalist and elephant researcher Douglas Chadwick sums it up: "As long as elephants are free to wander, they only stir the habitat they use. But they can hammer an environment when confined." Kruger holds 80 percent of the nation's elephants. The park's carrying capacity has been set at 7,500 elephants. To maintain this, rangers typically cull 300 to 400 a year. Often the first to be culled are known crop raiders. Many parts of Kruger are surrounded by fences. However, even South Africa cannot afford elephant-proof fencing. A hungry and determined elephant will plow right through any barriers to raid nearby crops.

Involving the local community

The park is trying to change with the times. According to Chris Marais, a park employee, "The old idea of how to run a park was: put up a big fence, get big guns and keep the neighbors and their cattle out." This obviously fosters contempt from local people. So today steps are being taken to make sure that the park's neighbors have a vested interest in it. Hiring local people as guides and caretakers was the first step. In addition, park funds have established medical clinics and helped out with irrigation projects, and native people are allowed to sell their crafts to tourists within the park.

It is uncertain whether these burgeoning efforts can make up for several centuries of land misuse. Until such time as their native habitats can be sufficiently restored, elephants will be forced onto whatever land is available, whether it be in a limited natural preserve or at a zoo on the other side of the world.

4

Elephants in Captivity

WHILE THE ELEPHANT'S habitat continues to shrink in the wilds of Africa and Asia, some scientists believe that one of the last hopes for a stable population maintained in completely protected surroundings lies in the captive breeding and education programs that take place in zoos and parks throughout the world. Zoos foster an awareness of wildlife and wild habitats that would be hard for most people to imagine growing up without. However, today the issue of animals in captivity is a hot one. At one extreme are animal rights activists who claim that there is no justifiable reason to keep any animals in captivity. Others, who now often refer to themselves as animal welfarists, consider zoos and parks to be a vital link in the conservation of endangered species.

Elephants are often at the center of this controversy. The public seems to have a genuine affection for these social and intelligent giants. The issue of such an enormous animal being confined to less than enormous surroundings raises the hackles of many animal activists. The irony is that unlike most other zoo animals, elephants have been "domesticated" by humans, or trained in captivity, for thousands of years. They have been handled much like horses and oxen for tasks including building, hauling, logging, and even warfare. The relationship between humans and elephants goes back a very long way. According to African studies professor Kenneth Wylie, Sanskrit texts dating back to 1500 B.C. describe

an already ancient tradition of elephant "taming," for warfare, entertainment, and industry.

Hannibal used elephants to defeat the Romans in 218 B.C. The elephants terrified the Roman horses.

Logging elephants

One ancient elephant service that is still practiced today is the use of Asian elephants as work animals in commercial construction, logging, and agriculture. Today their chief function remains as logging animals. In fact, their usefulness in this capacity in some cases seems to be in their own interest. The influx of Western culture, machinery, and values into southern Asia has led to the massive clear-cutting of forests. Elephants used in place of heavy machinery provide several benefits to their habitat as well as their employers.

Unlike heavy machinery, elephants don't need massive roads carved into the forest. They travel along narrow, existing paths. When large roads are cut through the forests, they not only destroy huge tracts of plant and animal life, but they also provide a ready-made access route for poachers, as well as slash-and-burn farmers, to travel deep into the forests. In addition, elephants run on cheap renewable fuel: grass. Logging machinery runs on petroleum, which is expensive, causes pollution, and is not a renewable resource. Lastly, when the logging machines reach their destination in the forest, they must veer off the roads, crashing through even more brush. These machines typically travel on tank tread, which pulverizes the ground, leaving little chance of regrowth. An elephant's four feet do far less damage.

The problem with elephants, however, is that they cannot clear as much timber in as short a time as a machine. The solution, according to Michael Schmidt, a veterinarian and member of IUCN's Asian Elephant Specialist Group, is to keep as many elephants as possible employed in this industry. It would be just as cost-effective to keep and maintain the necessary number of elephants, says Schmidt, as it would to have adequate machinery. Currently, there are thirteen thousand to sixteen thousand working elephants in Asia, about 25 percent of the wild population. Unfortunately, even the countries with the best elephant management programs are only able to breed about half of the elephants they need each year to stay in business. The rest have to be collected from the wild. The practice of annually collecting a few hundred ten- to twenty-year-old elephants from the wild has gone on for centuries in most of these countries.

Elephants have been used as work animals since ancient times. Here, an elephant moves logs in Sri Lanka.

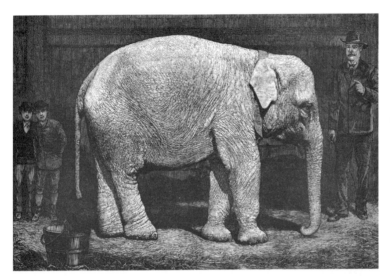

An albino circus elephant is portrayed in this nineteenth-century lithograph. The first elephants in North America were imported for circuses.

Today, though, there simply aren't enough elephants left in the wild to continue removing them for logging. With the assistance of Western researchers, more attempts are being made to improve the logger's captive breeding rates, most successfully in Myanmar, where an average of one hundred calves are born each year. This figure does not yet equal the number of elephants that die or retire each year, but continued increases could make the elephant industry self-sustaining within a few years.

North America's elephants

The first elephants in North America were imported as performers by traveling circuses. As the popularity of circuses grew in the United States, more circuses could afford to purchase both African and Asian elephants. These animals were a proven crowd pleaser, and by the early 1900s most successful circuses had at least one. People came from miles around when the circus was in town to marvel at these incredible hulking beasts, which were unlike anything they had ever seen. Today the term "circus elephant" often elicits a very different reaction. Animal rights groups have spent a lot of time and money spreading the word that elephants don't belong in captivity—especially not in circuses, where many feel they are treated cruelly.

Children take advantage of a typical fair adventure—the elephant ride. Many animal rights activists have worked to disband this practice, which they believe is demeaning to the elephant.

A more enlightened approach

Until recently, most zoos were very much like stationary circuses. The average zoo of fifty years ago was a large menagerie of as many different animals as could be collected and caged. Little attention was paid to the behavioral enrichment of the animals or even to proper veterinary care, much less conservation issues. Today the average zoo prides itself not on how many animals and cages it can fit on its grounds, but instead on its ability to provide the most healthy and enriching animal environments possible. Many people see zoos today as a modern-day ark, providing endangered animals with a last safe haven from the ravages of their diminishing wild environments. Zoos affect the status of the world's elephant population in several important ways.

Wildlife education

So much attention is focused today on the conservation of endangered species and habitats. Where did this interest develop from? According to Robert Hoage, a zoologist at the National Zoological Park, this interest stems from the public's ability to see animals live and up close. Hoage claims that "zoos can impress upon the public how marvelous animals are and why we don't want a world without them." Without zoos and animal parks, the average American would never get to see an elephant. It is this close, personal connection with an animal that often stimulates people to become interested and concerned about their fate.

Wildlife education and the stimulation of public interest in conservation issues are becoming a major focus of many parks and zoos in the United States today. Most zoos have some type of outreach program that offers classes on, for example, junior zoology or research apprenticeships. Many zoos that house elephants present informative and entertaining shows. The old circus-style shows, with their emphasis on tricks and flashy performances, are being replaced by more constructive presentations geared toward heightening people's awareness of these majestic creatures—their biology, behavior, and struggle for survival.

In some zoos, a person can even touch or ride an elephant. Elephant rides are still a topic of controversy, as some people see it as demeaning to such an intelligent animal. Many elephant handlers believe that these rides are actually a healthy outlet for their charges. Lee Simmons, executive director of the Omaha Zoo, feels that working animals are "happier and healthier than the guy who is just lying in the back of the yard." In fact, some elephants apparently enjoy the activity. Dave Tuttle of the Jacksonville Zoo, says that "Ellie [a twenty-five-year-old female] looked forward to giving rides and liked it. Some days she would be standing at the gate waiting to go give the rides." While rides may be an important factor in keeping an elephant alert and stimulated, Tuttle says that the chief benefit is the increased appreciation a person gets from such close contact. "If you stand by the rides and listen to adults and children getting off an elephant, they're really mesmerized by it. You can tell people have a new appreciation for the animal and the next time they see 'Save Elephants, Don't Use Ivory,' they're going to pay more attention to that message."

Breeding

One of the most compelling arguments for the necessity of zoos and animal parks is the need for a stable breeding environment for animals whose wild habitats are shrinking and on the verge of collapse. If the Asian forests and African savannas disappear, replaced by cities and plantations, captive-bred zoo elephants will be the last of their kind. However, breeding elephants is no simple matter. For many years, the average zoo had no unrelated elephants to breed, and inbreeding was the only alternative. In 1979, though, Katherine Ralls, a research scientist at the National Zoo in Washington, D.C., demonstrated to the zoo community, using a computer model, that if no changes were made, zoo animals would become so inbred in the coming years that they could not possibly sustain a healthy population. Her model went on to show that in as little as 150 years, most captive animal populations would die out completely as a result of this inbreeding.

Zoo directors and curators took notice and then took action in the formation of the Species Survival Plan (SSP). The American Zoo and Aquarium Association (AZA) formulated an SSP for each of the captive species it deemed most endangered. Each individual SSP outlines, in great detail, a breeding program designed to increase successful births and decrease inbreeding. A complete list of the location and histories of every SSP animal in North American zoos is kept by the plan's studbook keeper. This person is responsible for arranging trades between zoos to ensure compatible and genetically diverse breeding. If an SSP studbook keeper informs a zoo that its elephant would be best matched for breeding at another zoo three thousand miles away, the zoo will usually comply and trade its animal. All accredited zoos in the nation are active participants in the SSP, and refusal to cooperate is rare.

Few elephants born in captivity

Elephants develop and mature to breeding age very slowly. In addition, their gestational period (or length of pregnancy) is almost two years, and they are very picky about whom they will breed with. These factors have contributed to a less than overwhelming success rate for captive elephant breeding. However, things are improving. The first captive elephant was born in this country in 1880. From that time until 1962, there were only eight other births. Since 1962 there have been 101 more, 50 percent of which occurred in the last ten years. By keeping detailed records and sharing them with other members of the zoo community, captive elephant breeding has begun to advance. Unfortunately, all these successes have been with Asian elephants only. Thus far African elephants have bred in captivity only on very rare occasions. This is due to a

Mother and daughter elephants at the Houston Zoo reach out with their trunks to their trainer, who holds a treat. Enlightened zoo practices have greatly improved conditions for all animals, including elephants.

number of factors, including fewer African elephants in zoos throughout this country (since they are more difficult to obtain and handle) and their slower maturity rate.

The Elephant Managers Association

The question remains: Does having elephants in captivity help their wild cousins or hurt them? Some animal rights groups still contend that it is impossible to provide an elephant with anything close to a natural and healthy life in captivity. People for the Ethical Treatment of Animals (PETA), for example, takes the position that all elephants should be freed and returned to the wild. However, Robert Hoage, a zoologist at the National Zoo, argues, "PETA assumes that there is a wild that the animals can go back to. We believe that the wild itself is going extinct." Many activist groups feel that even the commendable efforts of America's leading zoos do not make up for all the other elephants that receive poor care and are kept in smaller, substandard exhibits. Most zookeepers agree that some elephants are treated improperly, but they point out that it is usually the result of a lack of proper training on the part of the keepers.

In 1988 the zoo community decided to do something about this. Handlers and keepers from around the country got together to form the Elephant Managers Association, or EMA. The EMA is a nonprofit organization whose goal is "to improve and professionalize elephant management practices, which will improve management and treatment of elephants." Almost every zoo or park with elephants that is accredited by the American Zoo and Aquarium Association (AZA) has at least one representative in the EMA. There are still several different philosophies about how to best handle elephants: Some believe a hands-on approach is the only effective way to train an elephant, while others argue that limited contact is far safer and just as productive. Each of the EMA members brings his or her perspective to the group.

They have annual conferences and publish several journals each year. Through the efforts of this group, even the smallest zoos now have access to all the available training, husbandry, and breeding techniques. Dave Blasko, president of the EMA, feels strongly about the importance of sharing knowledge: "It is important that we progress from where we were 30 years ago."

Well trained and treated with care

Captive elephant breeding is a science that will naturally benefit from keeper communication. With the slow reproductive rate of these animals, even the most progressive zoos only have the opportunity to witness elephant breeding and rearing on a handful of individuals. Today EMA members have access to detailed records of just about every captive birth in North America. Blasko is also the manager of the Elephant Encounter at Marine World Africa USA, an animal park in northern California. Marine World has a large collection of African and Asian elephants that are handled, walked, ridden, bathed, and medicated, in close contact with people, on a daily basis. These elephants appear to have a very satisfactory existence, rarely demonstrating any of the violent tendencies often depicted on the evening news. Blasko feels that his elephants are well behaved because they are well trained and, consequently, they get to enjoy a fair degree of freedom in their daily routine. According to Blasko, "The better trained [an elephant] is, the more freedom it has. A human child that is poorly trained, and poorly behaved can't even go out to a public restaurant." The goal of the EMA is to see all elephants in captivity well trained and able to live as comfortable a life as possible.

Keeping animals in captivity may always be a topic for controversy. However, one thing does seem clear: Elephants are currently fighting a battle for survival in their ancient habitats. If the battle is lost, captive populations will be this planet's only hope of preserving the species.

5

The Future of the Elephant

MUCH HAS BEEN learned during the past quarter century about the biology, behavior, and preservation of the elephant. Perhaps the most fundamental questions still remaining are: Are there sufficiently compelling reasons to save this species? and, if so, Is it already too late? To the average Western conservationist, the answer seems clear: Of course the elephant should be saved. However, many of the local people living alongside wild elephant habitat would disagree.

The reality of living among elephants can often be surprisingly harsh. The majority of native people in elephant habitat exist as subsistence farmers. In other words, they live by raising crops and livestock to feed their families. These people depend on their agriculture for their very survival. Local farmers whose entire crops have been wiped out by hungry elephants have good reason to harbor animosity toward the animals. The lives of some African and Asian people consist of being terrorized by marauding herds of elephants. People are trampled, homes are destroyed, and entire farms are ravaged.

In addition, localized overpopulation of elephants in certain wildlife reserves has led to mass destruction of both flora and fauna. Confined to one area, elephants will quickly cause extensive damage to trees and shrubs, as well as all the animals that depend on the foliage. This problem of too many elephants and too little space has led to the destruction

An African elephant resorts to eating dry twigs during a drought. In some areas, elephant overpopulation has led to the destruction of forests and woodlands.

of forests and woodlands from Zaire to South Africa. The loss of habitat, in turn, can lead to the extinction of other neighboring animals. The bushbuck and lesser kudu, for example, have died out completely in Kenya's Amboseli National Park as a result of elephant destruction.

Elephants do appear to be destructive by design. However, their destructive tendencies are, in fact, an important part of a larger picture. The elephant is what biologists refer to as a keystone species. Defined as an animal that has the capacity to shape or modify its habitat, keystone species are vital links in the ecological chain of their environments. For example, in rain forest areas, elephants are responsible for knocking down trees, which permits more sunlight to pass through the canopy and reach the ground. This spurs the growth of rich ground cover, on which many forest inhabitants depend for survival. It is also the mechanism by which new trees are spawned. In drier areas, elephants tear up the ground in search of water. This often angers farmers, but it also can provide the only available water source to countless other species during a drought. In addition, elephants open paths through thickets and are responsible for distributing seeds, many of which must pass through the elephant's gut in order to germinate.

Ecosystems as a whole depend largely on their keystone species for survival. Smaller, less well known, and perhaps less attractive species of insects, rodents, and vegetation have to ride the coattails of the neighboring "charismatic megafauna." This term refers to large, attractive, and well-liked animal species that people donate their time and money to save. Elephants fall into this category, and through efforts to save them, countless other less "popular" species are saved as well. For example, the amount of wild space required to sustain just two elephants will also protect the habitat of eight bushbucks and forty rock hyraxes, not to mention millions of insects (which some biologists argue are the backbone of any ecosystem). According to David Western, currently the director of Kenya's Wildlife Services, "Loss of elephants could trigger an avalanche of extinctions."

Natural selection

Another argument against saving the dwindling elephant population is the idea that these animals are dying off as a result of the environmental system of checks and balances, described by Darwin as natural selection. The reality is that the extinction of the elephant is anything but natural. Normal extinction is a process that occurs gradually over a period of tens of thousands of years. Elephant numbers have dropped to levels never before witnessed in their long history. Even at the turn of the twentieth century, elephant populations were still at stable, self-sustaining numbers. Scientists estimate that if current trends continue, the wild elephant could be wiped out completely in another few decades. This rapid die-off is less than a blink in the eye of time and is directly related to the adverse effects of overwhelming human population growth and industrialization. In general, it is estimated that extinction rates have increased by about 1,000 percent since humans entered the world. Proponents of protecting elephants and other endangered species argue that the human gift of higher reasoning, which has allowed us to dominate our world, brings with it knowledge of the consequences of our actions and the subsequent burden of taking responsibility for those actions. In short, conservationists believe that humans have caused the elephant's current predicament, and, therefore, humans should take an active role in fixing the problem.

The wild spaces

Today there are several thousand public and private wildlife reserves of one type or another. Many of these are located in African and Asian territories that contain indigenous elephant populations. That's the good news. The bad news is that the science of habitat preservation is very new, and many of these reserves are grossly inadequate to sustain a viable population of elephants. Of course, some are better than others, but most wildlife reserves are small isolated pockets, or islands, of habitat. These individual islands are cut off from the rest of the elephant's natural range and usually do not provide sufficient room to travel or food to eat.

There are several inherent problems with this type of reserve. In the short term, elephants confined to small territories will invariably wreak havoc on the local landscape. As ecologists have shown, when elephants are allowed to roam free, their destruction of trees and shrubs is a necessary part of the growth cycle in an ecosystem. However, when their migration patterns are restricted, they will repeatedly hammer the same area again and again. This creates an unsustainable habitat for not only the elephants, but all the other flora and fauna in the area, including humans.

In the long term, these isolated habitat islands prevent the exchange of genetic material between herds. The only way for any species to survive and thrive is to constantly stir the gene pool. Continued inbreeding over generations can cause a host of problems for a species, from poor physical constitution to sterility. Elephants achieve genetic diversity and the healthy growth of their species by having

ROTHCO
ORIGINAL

"FRANKLY, PROFESSOR, I THINK WE'RE THE ONLY
ENDANGERED SPECIES AROUND HERE!"

the males leave their family groups at maturity to seek out and mate with females of unrelated herds. When they are unable to leave their "island" habitats, this cannot happen, and inbreeding occurs.

The problem of habitat fragmentation can also arise accidentally. Many elephants still exist on unprotected wild lands. When a local town decides to erect a village or farm in the middle of an elephant's range, "fault zones" are created. The elephants are cut off from their extended family, food, and water sources. If they attempt to cross the newly developed areas, they usually leave a path of destruction in their wake, eating crops or trampling homes. This situation is sometimes referred to as "pocketed herds." Very often local people are not even aware that they have trapped a group of elephants in their territory. The elephants may stay hidden in untouched land during the day and come out to feed only at night. People are often surprised at the number of pocketed herds living in close proximity to human settlements. Large numbers of elephants living so near to human settlements can obviously be very dangerous. For example, a brush fire in India in 1994 caused a pocketed herd to stampede through several nearby villages, crushing six people and damaging crops. Though the elephants were there first, they are depicted by locals as a threat to their welfare and often systematically killed off.

Habitat corridors

The solution to both pocketed herds and isolated wildlife reserves would appear to be the construction of habitat corridors, through which the elephants could travel to other areas. In the case of the pocketed elephants, nations such as India, Indonesia, and Sri Lanka have been successful at permanently relocating herds through the use of one-way channels. According to John Seidensticker, of the World Bank, the key to a successful relocation plan for pocketed elephants has three parts: The elephants must have a suitable prearranged place to go, a way to get there, and no easy route by which to return.

As for the small protected island reserves, IUCN's Asian Elephant Specialist Group—along with a number of other organizations—has come up with detailed plans for sustainable two-way migration corridors. Unlike the relocation plans for accidentally pocketed animals, these corridors should be permanent and well maintained. Creating a series of natural channels between reserves would allow the elephants to move back and forth as the need arises. Plans for these corridors should recognize established elephant migration routes and provide them with maintenance and protection from development. The existence of these corridors should minimize conflicts between humans and elephants, as well as provide natural exchanges of genetic material between herds. One problem with this plan is the need for these corridors to cross national borders. Elephants do not recognize the invisible lines humans have drawn across their habitat. However, the governments of the world do and are often unwilling to cooperate with neighbors in these matters. As the problem continues to gain international attention on a grand scale, many nations are doing their best to put aside political differences in the best interests of the elephants.

Creating boundaries

Another problem with many reserves is the way in which the parks' boundaries are established. Some nations favor extensive fencing to keep the animals inside, for their own safety. This can be expensive, and few fences are effective against a determined elephant. Some parks utilize deep moats or ditches around their preserves. This, again, is not always an effective barrier against an elephant, as they have been observed systematically filling in ditches with dirt to create land bridges to freedom. According to Seidensticker, these types of physical barriers are essentially a challenge to a hungry elephant. He feels that a more productive solution lies in creating large natural boundaries around the park that have zero appeal to the elephant. One method would be to establish areas of large grassland that have been heavily overgrazed by domestic livestock and, therefore, lack any suitable shade. These zones, which would act as natural barriers between elephants and people, have been used successfully in some parts of Sri Lanka. This concept is compatible with the larger scale plans of the United Nation's Man and Biosphere Program (MAB). This program describes parks of the future as consisting of a fully protected core area, surrounded by one or more buffer zones in which human needs are taken into account. As the rings or zones progress outward, there can be increasing levels of human activity. The innermost buffer zones may be reserved for noninvasive research and tourism. The outer rings could be utilized by local people for wood gathering, light hunting, and even settlements. Ideally, the boundaries of these zones would be determined by a combined effort of scientists, wildlife managers, and local people. The Nilgiri ecosystem in India is a good example of an MAB site. Methods such as these, which incorporate the needs of local people, can go a long way to ease the tension between humans and elephants.

Making elephants into assets

In parts of the world where native people depend on the limited resources of their environment for survival, many humans see elephant preserves as giant wastes of space. National parks are often viewed with hostility by neighboring rural people. Many poverty-stricken farmers believe the land could be put to better use for agriculture and cattle grazing, and they refer to the parks as the "white man's garden." Natives often view their government's prohibition of land use as oppression and believe they should be free to do with the land as they please. These feelings are deep-rooted and cause even more friction in an already difficult struggle. One example of the local attitude toward national parks was clearly demonstrated, as apartheid dissolved, when a large number of Namibians celebrated independence from South African rule by racing into the Etosha National Park with guns and trucks and proceeding to poach as much wild game as they could. Obviously, the attitude of local inhabitants will need to change if these conservation efforts are to have any chance of succeeding. The most important step will be finding ways to make these preserves and their wild inhabitants beneficial to the neighboring villages, rather than a source of enmity.

Zimbabwe has taken steps toward these ends by establishing a new program that tangibly links wildlife preservation with local human survival. The program is called CAMPFIRE—Communal Areas Management Programme for Indigenous Resources—and involves granting local people ownership of their wildlife. They are encouraged to promote game hunting, tourism, and wildlife photography in their home regions. The income from these exploits is then given to local town councils, who can decide for themselves how to allocate the money (for schools, medicine, food, and other services). The only stipulation is that the wildlife is managed in a sustainable fashion. One percent of local elephant populations may be hunted, and these numbers are strictly enforced. The average rural family of eight in Zimbabwe exists on about $150 a year.

Tourists engage in a safari by elephant in Botswana. Some countries are encouraging such tourism to help raise money to support their conservation efforts.

Hunters will pay as much as $12,000 per elephant. This money goes a very long way for the local people.

The idea behind giving the native people stewardship over their own land is to foster a desire to protect wildlife for the sake of their own preservation—the primary concern of poverty-stricken societies. The program is still new but appears to be working. Communities are assisted in developing the skills and self-confidence necessary to implement advanced projects, such as constructing irrigation systems, and developing community-wide shareholder companies. According to Brian Child, senior ecologist in CAMPFIRE, the number of elephants killed by local people for damaging crops has dropped significantly. In the Gokwe community, elephant deaths dropped from forty-five to three in just three years. In other areas, people have even abandoned their traditional homes and centralized their settlements to create more open spaces for wildlife. Programs such as these will help reduce the "us or them" attitude that hampers many conservation programs throughout the world.

A question of numbers

While the elephant species as a whole continues to decline, local populations in some isolated reserves are swelling to dangerous levels. Each area of protected habitat has a maximum carrying capacity of wildlife it can support comfortably. When this number is exceeded, the health of the entire ecosystem begins to fail. Some reserves in southern Africa have had expanding elephant populations for years. Even some of the poorer nations of the east coast have had difficulty controlling the numbers since the end of the ivory trade in 1989. What to do about this overpopulation is a topic for heated disagreement in both Africa and Asia.

Until recently, the favored method for controlling elephant numbers has been culling, or systematically killing off, portions of the population. Some environmentalists believe this goes against the grain of everything they have worked to achieve and find it an unacceptable course. This opinion is not shared by the local officials, who must deal with the problems overcrowded elephants cause. "We are not a zoo to be preserved for the international community. People also live here," says Seeiso Liphuko, secretary of Botswana's National Conservation Strategy. Elephant numbers in Botswana have been on the rise for years. The population is currently estimated at sixty thousand and growing 3 to 5 percent each year. Botswana has a respectable conservation record, devoting .31 percent of its national budget to environmental issues (this is about twice the percentage spent in the United States). Despite crop raiding and forest destruction, Botswana had a freeze on elephant culling from 1983 to 1992. In 1992 the country was forced to begin the program again.

Alternative to cullings

That year a severe drought threatened to wipe out many animals and people in and near Zimbabwe's Gonarezhov National Park. The park found it necessary to cull about two thousand elephants. According to Rowan Martin, chief ecologist of the Zimbabwean National Parks Department, it just doesn't make sense not to cull when their numbers are swelling and people are going hungry. This practice would not only ease the pressure the drought had put on the environment, but the meat from the culled animals could be distributed to the local people, who were starving.

There are alternatives to culling still in the experimental stages. To reduce the number of animals it needed to cull during the '92 drought, Zimbabwe called on the services of Clem Coetzee for help. Coetzee was a well-known game relocator but had little practice at moving full-grown elephants. He was able to devise new transport methods for the huge creatures, which allowed him to relocate about 300 individuals to safety. The next year Coetzee was brought back and, with improved techniques, managed to move another 670 elephants.

The practice of game translocation involves moving animals from crowded, unsustainable habitats to areas where these same animals are scarce and in danger of dying off completely. This conservation method is obviously far more difficult, expensive, and time-consuming than culling. However, some areas have had success with it. South Africa's Natal Parks Board has been engaging in this practice since 1962 and has moved over a hundred thousand animals (including some elephants). Most of what they move becomes breeding stock for game farms. A growing number of landowners are moving away from farming and toward converting their land into wildlife reserves to be utilized by tourists and game hunters. According to the Natal Parks Board, "Animals moved from various Natal Parks have produced more than a million offspring." Some groups don't agree with relocating animals to areas where they will be bred for game hunting. However, the fact remains that in the Transvaal region of South Africa alone, there are over 6 million acres of these private game reserves, which is larger than the entire Kruger National Park. In addition, there are over 1.7 million acres of private nature reserve. When combined with government protected areas, this means that about 30 percent of the province is sectioned off as sustainable habitat for wildlife. The ethics of hunting animals is a topic for debate that will go on for many years, but for now, the existence of this vast network of reserves will help to ensure a place for elephants to live and breed.

Studying parasite loads

Culling is still necessary and widespread throughout localized areas in both Africa and Asia. New methods are being developed to help determine the maximum wildlife carrying capacity for individual ecosystems. In the past, rough estimates were based on the conflicting research of biologists, who rated the environment in often subjective ways. Today one of the more scientific methods involves studying parasite loads of the local wildlife. Almost all wild animals live with parasites. As they get old or sick, their bodies weaken and the parasites are able to take hold more easily. By observing changes in the parasite load of a herd, biologists can now judge the relative health of its members. This provides them with more accurate measures of just how many elephants can live in a given space. Kruger National Park estimates its carrying capacity at about 7,500 elephants. Each year their population grows by 4 to 5 percent, and, as a result, they must cull several hundred elephants annually. In 1994, 577 elephants were slated for elimination. However, the park agreed to sell 158 of these to Coetzee for $2,142 each. With the added financial backing of the International Fund for Animal Welfare (IFAW), Coetzee was able to move these animals to eight different private reserves. The IFAW gave Coetzee over $142,000 to cover the transportation costs, with the stipulation that none of the animals went to hunting reserves.

Birth control

Another very new and experimental attempt to control elephant numbers in overcrowded areas is the use of chemical birth control on wild elephant populations. Joyce Poole, a well-known elephant researcher, heads up a birth control vaccine project in Kenya. Poole feels that it is not right to "go in and start gunning down elephants without looking for some kind of alternative." In 1994 she and a team of wildlife managers went to Sweetwaters Rhino Sanctuary and, using helicopters and tranquilizers, managed to immobilize three adult female elephants long enough to properly inject the vaccine. These elephants had radio collars placed around their necks so their movements could be tracked. Unfortunately, preliminary results of the procedure are difficult to assess. Elephants only cycle once every four months and take twenty-two months to complete a pregnancy. Poole thinks the initial results seem promising and the research continues.

Captive populations

The attitudes and advances in captive elephant husbandry are also changing dramatically. One new source of hope for elephants lies in the advances currently being made with breeding through artificial insemination. To date, this process has been successful only with small numbers of domestic elephant herds in Myanmar. It is not easy to accomplish, as female elephants ovulate only three times a year, and the methods by which handlers determine an elephant's current state of fertility are inaccurate at best. There are no external signs of ovulation. The only way to tell is by measuring progesterone levels in the female's blood. In Myanmar, this presents logistical problems since the labs needed to analyze the blood samples are often located far from the elephants themselves. When the timing is right, trained elephants will accept the administration of previously collected semen. So far, no successful method of freezing live sperm has been developed. It must be collected and used within a short period of time. American zoos are working to perfect techniques of accurately timing ovulation and implantation. In addition, work is being done to perfect the freezing techniques needed to establish large sperm banks, sometimes referred to as frozen zoos. Once these banks have been developed, it will be possible to impregnate a female elephant in a zoo in California with the sperm of a healthy bull from across the world. This will do much to preserve the genetic diversity necessary for the continuation of any species.

Most elephant advocates saw the ivory ban in 1989 as a major success in the war against extinction. Some nations, however, feel that the international ban on trade in elephant parts was an overreaction to unsettling discoveries presented at the time. Several southern African nations, whose elephant population is continuing to increase, argue that there is nothing wrong with utilizing wildlife in a sustainable fashion, the way native Africans and Asians have done for thousands of years. According to Zimbabwe officials, many Western conservationists believe wildlife should be conserved solely for its aesthetic and ethical value. They argue that this preservationist view of wildlife comes from strongly held personal convictions, based on subjective value judgments that should not be imposed on starving people who do not share these beliefs. The renewal of this trade would bring in much-needed funds for local people. It would go a long way toward providing food and shelter, as well as making the elephant populations a valuable asset to the local inhabitants, who would then stand to benefit from the continued survival of the species. Otherwise, they say, the elephants remain pests in the eyes of the locals, and the situation is reduced to a simple contest for space and survival between man and beast.

Controlled trade allowed

Of course, food and money for starving people goes a long way in influencing decisions. In 1992, $1.6 million worth of stockpiled ivory was collected and now sits in warehouses, unable to be sold. One of the major topics at the June '97 CITES conference was whether or not to allow southern African nations to sell the five hundred to six hundred tons of stockpiled ivory in their possession. Zimbabwe, Botswana, and Namibia went on record as opposing the continuation of the ban. They proposed a measure that would downgrade the African elephant to Appendix II, listing it as a threatened species, and allow controlled trade in ivory, as well as in meat and skins. This measure was at first voted down, but after some changes it was passed on a second vote. Under the new ruling, the elephants of Botswana, Namibia, and Zimbabwe only will be reclassified to Appendix II as of October 1997. These countries will then have eighteen months to put strict regulatory protocols into place. In March 1999, if the proper controls are in place, these three nations—which have clearly shown an overpopulation of African elephants—will be permitted to resume legal trade in ivory and other elephant products.

Opponents of the decision claim that the starving people of these nations don't really stand to make that much money. According to ban proponents, during the 1980s, when trade was still legal and supposedly regulated, less than 10 percent of the income from ivory sales actually made it to the people. The rest went to smugglers, middlemen, and into the pockets of officials. Even the sale of just the stockpiled ivory would open the door to several years of illegal poaching, as most buyers will have no way of determining whether the ivory they are buying came from a warehouse in Botswana or a pregnant female from Kenya. Trade supporters claim that new techniques of DNA and chemical composition testing will allow authorities to determine ivory's area of origin. This may be the case in several years, but for now these new methods are still not perfected. The DNA samples can only be obtained from the tissue at the base of the tusk, so cut or worked ivory could not be tested. The chemical trace test can be conducted on any piece of ivory, no matter how small. However, the chemical traces that are located are supposed to be linked to the diet of localized elephant herds, and until the exact diet and chemical composition of every herd in Africa can be categorized, this will not be a viable method for illegal ivory detection.

Ecotourism

The poorer nations also argue that the ecotourism industry is doing the job of bringing in money and making elephants into local assets. Tens of thousands of people come to the wildlife parks of Africa and Asia every year. They come to see the vast expanses of unspoiled natural habitat that no longer exists in most industrialized nations. Elephants, which are both extremely visible and awe-inspiring, are a major part of this attraction. Many native people are employed by these national parks directly or benefit from the constant flow of tourists who wish to buy their crafts and foods. In addition, a portion of most national park revenues go to the local communities, in the form of food, medicine, schooling, and housing. The question, then, is whether ecotourism alone will be enough. Does the sale of hunting licenses and elephant parts bring in enough extra income to make it worth the risk to the elephants and the increased policing efforts that would be required to control it?

Cooperation, it seems, will be the key to protecting elephants. The human inhabitants of the earth do not yet agree on any one moral stance toward the role this animal plays in the world. Some societies see it as sacred, others simply as a resource to be used. Each of these groups spends a vast amount of energy protecting their view of what the natural world should be. Many of these views are in direct conflict with one another. Political upheaval and warring environmental philosophies create enormous obstacles. Much of the energy spent on conservation efforts is directed at countering the "immoral," "impractical," or simply "incorrect" efforts of other groups. True progress cannot be achieved until the planet's dominant life-form, humans, can come to an agreement about which direction to move in. As one highly respected investigative journalist, Douglas Chadwick, points out in his book *The Fate of the Elephant*, "How can we hope to get along with other species, when we are doing so poorly at getting along with one another?" There is still time to secure a future for the elephant. However, if people decide the elephant is worth saving, they will have to hurry because the window of opportunity is getting smaller with each passing year.

A warden in Zimbabwe poses inside the state ivory warehouse. Many poor nations would like to be able to sell such ivory on the open market.

Glossary

allomothers: Elephant baby-sitters, usually sisters, aunts, or grandmothers.

artificial insemination: The practice of impregnating captive females with previously collected sperm.

charismatic megafauna: Large, attractive, well-liked animals that people are usually prone to help conserve.

CITES: Convention on the International Trade in Endangered Species. A regulatory group that decides through the mutual agreement of its members on international policies concerning trade in endangered species.

clear-cutting: Practice of felling all the trees in a section of forest at the same time.

culling: Thinning out an overcrowded population by organized killings.

ecosystem: A biologically balanced environment formed by the interaction of plants and animals.

ecotourism: The booming industry that provides nature-oriented vacations in national parks and reserves.

Elephas maximus: Scientific name for the Asian elephant.

endangered species: A plant or animal species that is nearing extinction.

fault zones: Areas created by human development that cut off elephants from native feeding and breeding grounds.

fitness: The measure of an animal's ability to reproduce itself.

forage: To search an environment for food.

genetic diversity: A healthy recombination of DNA, which allows a species to thrive and develop throughout time.

habitat: The locality or living place of a plant or animal.

herbivore: An animal that only eats plant material.

IUCN: International Union for the Conservation of Nature. Organization that conducts research and makes recommendations on conservation issues.

keystone species: An animal that has the ability to shape or modify its habitat.

Loxodonta africana: Scientific name for the African elephant.

MAB: Man and Biosphere Program. Type of nature reserve proposed by the United Nations that consists of a central protected core area surrounded by buffer zones.

Moeritherium: The first ancestor of the modern-day elephant: a small piglike creature.

musth: Period of sexual activity for male elephants, during which they are extremely aggressive and secrete a fluid from a gland near their eyes.

national park: An area of wild habitat protected from development by a nation's government.

poaching: Illegal hunting or removal from private or protected lands.

pocketed herds: Herds of elephants that have been trapped in isolated patches of forest by human development.

slash-and-burn farming: A method of farming whereby farmers burn a patch of forest to the ground, clearing a plot of land and providing the soil with natural fertilizer.

SSP: Species Survival Plan. A plan drawn up by the American Zoo and Aquarium Association to help ensure the future of selected species through tightly controlled captive breeding practices.

subsistence farming: Raising crops and livestock for the sole purpose of feeding oneself and one's family.

sustainable development: Utilizing an area's resources without destroying them.

Organizations to Contact

African Wildlife Foundation
1717 Massachusetts Ave., NW
Washington, DC 20036
(202) 265-8393
website: www.awf.org

With offices in Washington, most of their staff is based in Africa. Works on grassroots programs with park managers and communities to safeguard wildlife and wilderness areas.

David Sheldrick Wildlife Trust
P.O. Box 15555
Nairobi, Kenya

An organization that raises and cares for orphaned elephants in Africa.

Elephant Managers Association
c/o John Lehnhardt
The National Zoological Park
Washington, DC 20008
website: www.Indyzoo.com/EMA/

The EMA is an organization that promotes the proper care and husbandry of captive elephants in North America and throughout the world. Its members include representatives from most U.S. elephant facilities. They publish several journals each year and hold annual conferences.

National Wildlife Federation
1412 16th St., NW
Washington, DC 20036
(202) 797-6800
website: www.nwf.org

The NWF attempts to advance commonsense conservation policies through advocacy, education, and litigation in concert with affiliate groups across the country and throughout the world. This group also publishes several informative, award-winning magazines, such as *International Wildlife*.

The Tusk Fund
115 Ebury St.
London SW192U
United Kingdom
Tel.—0171 924-4347

The Tusk Fund seeks to protect wild areas in Africa for wildlife as well as the community through education and community wildlife programs.

UK Elephant Group
Will Travers
Cherry Tree Cottage
Coldharbour, Surrey RH5 6HA
United Kingdom
Tel.—0306 713350

An alliance of twelve conservation and animal welfare organizations. Affiliated groups include Elefriends, Environmental Investigation Agency, Greenpeace, and International Wildlife Coalition.

United Nations Environment Programme (UNEP)
DC2-0803
United Nations
New York, NY 10017
(212) 963-8093
website: www.unep.org

UNEP's mandate is to provide leadership and encourage partnership in caring for the environment by inspiring, informing, and enabling nations and peoples to improve their quality of life without compromising that of future generations. They are very active participants in a wide variety of international research and action plans.

World Wildlife Fund
1250 24th St., NW
Washington, DC 20037
(202) 293-4800
website: www.wwf.org

Established in 1961, the WWF is one of the most well known conservation groups in the world. They help to create and protect wildlife reserves throughout the world. They develop public education programs, investigate poaching and smuggling, and attempt to reconcile human needs with conservation through research and active programs.

Suggestions for Further Reading

Douglas Chadwick, "A Place for Parks in the New South Africa," *National Geographic*, July 1996.

Roger L. DiSilvestro, *The African Elephant: Twilight in Eden*. New York: John Wiley & Sons, 1991.

Jonathan Fisher, "To Ban or Not to Ban?" *International Wildlife*, May/June 1997.

Dan Freeman, *Elephants: The Vanishing Giants*. London: Bison Books Limited, 1980.

Leonard Lee Rue, *Elephants: A Portrait of the Animal World*. Leicester, UK: Magna Books, 1994.

Jeheskel Shoshani, ed., *Elephants: Majestic Creatures of the Wild*. Emmaus, PA: Rodale Press, 1992.

Geoffrey C. Ward, "India's Wildlife Dilemma," *National Geographic*, May 1992.

Works Consulted

Richard and Karen Barnes, "You Can't See the Elephant for the Trees," *Wildlife Conservation*, March/April 1990.

Janet Trowbridge Bohlen, "Africa's Ivory War," *Defender's Magazine*, March/April 1989.

Felicity Brooks, *Protecting Endangered Species*. Tulsa, OK: EDC Publishing, 1990.

Victoria Butler, "Elephants by the Truckload," *International Wildlife*, July/August 1995.

Douglas H. Chadwick, *The Fate of the Elephant*. San Francisco: Sierra Club Books, 1992.

Brian Child, "The Elephant as a Natural Resource: A Perspective from Zimbabwe," *Wildlife Conservation*, March/April 1993.

D. H. M. Cumming, R. F. Du Toit, and S. N. Stuart, *African Elephants & Rhinos: Status Survey and Conservation Action Plan*. Gland, Switzerland: IUCN, 1990.

Christopher Dickey, "The End of the Ivory Trail?" *Newsweek*, April 16, 1990.

Elephants and People: Zimbabwe's Alternative to the Ivory Trade Bans. Harare, Zimbabwe: The Zimbabwe Trust, 1990.

Dilip Ganguly, "Casualties Increase in India as Humans Battle Elephants," *San Jose Mercury News*, January 8, 1994.

Nicholas Georgiadis, "Fingerprinting Ivory," *Wildlife Conservation*, March/April 1993.

Peter Jackson, "Running Out of Room," *International Wildlife*, September/October 1986.

Debra Jordan, "Living Trophies," *The Animal's Voice Magazine*, vol. 2, no. 5, 1989.

Mike Keele, "North American Asian Elephant Birth Statistics: What Are the Numbers Telling Us?" *Journal of the Elephant Managers Association*, Summer 1996.

John Lehnhardt, "Working Elephants in Sri Lanka and Myanmar," *Elephant Managers Workshop*, 1995.

Nicholas Luard, *The Wildlife Parks of Africa*. Salem, NH: Salem House, 1986.

John Ramsey MacKinnon, *Animals of Asia: The Ecology of the Oriental Region*. New York: Holt, 1974.

Susan Okie, "Too Much of a Big Thing," *Washington Post*, 1994.

Ian Parker, *Ivory Crisis*. London: Chatto & Windus Ltd., 1983.

Jane Perlez, "Killing Elephants to Save People," *San Jose Mercury News*, July 5, 1992.

A Program to Save the African Elephant. Washington, DC: World Wildlife Fund, 1989.

Charles Santiapillai and Peter Jackson, *The Asian Elephant: An Action Plan for Its Conservation*. Gland, Switzerland: IUCN, 1990.

Michael J. Schmidt, "Working Elephants," *Scientific American*, January 1996.

Merlin E. Seamon, "Design of the Elephant Facility and Exhibit for the Jacksonville Zoological Gardens," *Journal of the Elephant Managers Association*, Spring 1995.

John Seidensticker, *Managing Elephant Depredation in Agricultural and Forestry Projects*. Washington, DC: The World Bank, 1984.

Lois Shagun, "Some Elephants Becoming Giant Dangers," *San Francisco Chronicle*, October 23, 1994.

David Western, "The Balance of Nature," *Wildlife Conservation*, March/April 1993.

James Younger, "Botswana Officials Want Elephant Killing to Be Accepted," *San Francisco Chronicle*, June 7, 1992.

Index

Picture Credits

About the Author

Stuart P. Levine received his bachelor's degree in behavioral psychology at the State University of New York at Binghamton, and his associate's degree in Exotic Animal Training and Management at Moorpark College in southern California.

After several years working as a counselor in psychiatric hospitals, he moved on to a career with animals. He spent several years working with a variety of animals at a park in northern California as a wildlife educator. He presented programs to grammar and middle schools throughout California, geared toward heightening young people's awareness of wildlife and wild habitats.

Though a native New Yorker, Levine and his bird, Bart, reside just outside San Francisco.